YOU wouldn't understand –
white teachers in multi-ethnic classrooms

YOU wouldn't understand –
white teachers in multi-ethnic classrooms

Sarah Pearce

Trentham Books
Stoke on Trent, UK and Sterling, USA

Trentham Books Limited
Westview House   22883 Quicksilver Drive
734 London Road   Sterling
Oakhill   VA 20166-2012
Stoke on Trent   USA
Staffordshire
England ST4 5NP

First published 2005

British Library Cataloguing-in-Publication Data
A catalogue record for this book is available from the British Library

ISBN-13: 978-1-85856-362-6
ISBN-10: 1-85856-362-3

Designed and typeset by Trentham Print Design Ltd, Chester and printed
in Great Britain by Cromwell Press Ltd, Trowbridge.

Contents

Acknowledgements

This book started life as a PhD thesis, and I remain grateful to Tony Brown, Tehmina Basit and especially Dave Heywood for their inspiration, support and guidance over the course of that project. I would also like to thank Arturo Trujillo for his belief, and for many helpful discussions on race and other matters. Thanks too to Ann-Marie Swain, Caroline Bailey, Anna Hazeldine, Victoria Armitage and Sarah Phillips for reading and commenting on earlier drafts. Many of the responses of students at Goldsmiths College to my ideas about white teachers have also fed into this book, and I am grateful to them.

Above all, I want to express my warm appreciation to the staff of St Matthew's Primary School. Though in the following pages I am occasionally critical of the views of some of the teachers at the school, I have never wavered in my respect and admiration for the commitment of the entire staff to the education and well-being of the children in their care.

Introduction

Books about race are usually about ethnic minority groups. And books about race and education are usually about ethnic minority children, and how race affects their lives. This book looks at these same issues, but from a different angle. It focuses on the race of the *majority* group, on white people. And its main concern is not the behaviour of the children but the teachers. In the UK, as in many other multi-ethnic Western countries, the vast majority of teachers are white. This book asks the questions, what impact does this have on the way teachers behave in the classroom, their relationships with children, and the way they see their role as teachers? And what consequences does it have for the children – of all ethnic groups – that they teach?

In looking for answers to these questions, the book takes a very personal perspective. It tells the story of five years in the early part of my career as a primary school teacher in which I struggled to understand how race – including my own – influenced my attitudes and my relationships in the classroom. The story is told through a series of diary extracts, in which I recorded incidents that occurred in the classroom, and conversations with children and colleagues around the school.

Why does the book focus only on *white* teachers? Why not all teachers who want to understand more about diversity in their communities and in their classrooms? Does it make any sense to say that the issues facing white teachers are any different from those that face all teachers? It is impossible to expect all white teachers to have the same attitudes or behave in the same way. But as this book demonstrates, being white does affect the way we see the world and our place within it, and has a significant impact on the way others see us.

Curiously, the fact that being white is a racial identity has not been widely accepted until very recently. Over the past thirty years, in which other racial labels have been discussed and debated in great detail in multi-ethnic Western societies, the term 'white' has remained in the background as a category – unexamined and therefore unchallenged. Many white people do not see themselves as belonging to a racial or ethnic group (Baumann, 1996; Frankenberg, 1993). For most, the word ethnic refers to ethnic minorities: white people rarely consider themselves to have an ethnicity. To be white is to be normal, neutral. In recent years this anomaly has begun to be called into question. It has been argued that being white influences the way you see the world – as being black does, though in rather different ways. For me, as for many white people, coming to see exactly how my whiteness affected my view of the world was a lengthy and difficult process, as this book illustrates.

The focus on whiteness may seem odd at a time when ethnicity and culture are increasingly recognised as more significant aspects of identity than skin colour. In the USA African-American has replaced black as the description for many, and in the UK African-Caribbean is increasingly preferred to black. These changes reflect the view that an emphasis on race, with its history of oppression, is less appropriate than an emphasis on ethnic and cultural identity, which is often seen as an identity we choose rather than one which is forced upon us (Blauner, 1994). Colour racism is increasingly regarded as over-simplistic and as ignoring the needs of groups whose primary identity is not represented by their skin colour, such as Muslims.

Yet there are important reasons for holding onto race as a concept, and for holding on to the notion of whiteness in particular. First, if we do away with the idea of race, we also do away with the idea of racism, and so lose the tools we need to tackle a phenomenon that shows no signs of disappearing. Thus, while ethnicity may become a more important element of our identities, we cannot afford to remove race entirely from our vocabulary (Goldberg, 2002). Second, we need to hold onto whiteness in particular, because the invisibility of whiteness as a racial identity has only just begun to be challenged. While other groups have been subjected to, and have subjected themselves to, detailed analysis, some white people have continued to believe they do not have any particular cultural standpoint. Holding on to whiteness as an idea enables us to challenge this invisibility, and to do away with the idea that white is a neutral, unproblematic identity (Frankenberg, 1997). The work that started years ago on exploring the terms black and Asian now needs to be done with the term white.

About the book

When I began to work at St Matthew's Primary School as a young white woman in my mid-twenties, I had little experience of living or working in ethnically diverse communities. I grew up and went to school in the far South West of England, an area with an overwhelmingly white population. I spent my early adulthood in mainly white environments, and, though I did my training in a large, ethnically diverse city, I received only one lecture on race and ethnic difference during my training, and both of my school placements were in overwhelmingly white schools. I spent my first two years as a newly qualified a teacher in another school in a mainly white area. Though I had chosen to train in that city in order to prepare myself to teach in a more diverse environment, and would have described myself as aware of race and racism in theory, it was not until I began work at St Matthew's that I began to reflect upon issues of race and ethnicity as issues that had anything to do with me as a white person. Just as gender has until recently been equated with women, and nothing to do with men, race is often seen as synonymous with ethnic minority issues and of little relevance to whites (Mac an Ghaill, 1999).

At St Matthew's, I was in a multi-ethnic environment for the first time. At the time, 90 per cent of the children at the school came from homes where the main language spoken was not English. Over 80 per cent of the school's intake was Muslim, the vast majority being of Pakistani or Bangladeshi origin. There were also several children from African or African-Caribbean backgrounds, and the remainder came from white, Indian or Vietnamese families. In contrast only one class teacher and three support staff were from ethnic minority groups when I began my study, though the number of support staff from minority groups had increased by the time I left the school five years later.

The school described in this book has in many ways disappeared. There have been changes to the curriculum, many of the staff have moved on, and almost all of the students whose voices are heard in the following pages are now well into their secondary education. I do not wish to claim that I have created an accurate portrait of St Matthew's Primary School: that was never my intention. What I have tried to do is capture what may be a more significant truth, and that is the truth about how I and my colleagues felt about race and about ethnic difference, and how those perceptions and pre-conceptions helped or hindered the teaching and learning process.

The diary

The book is based on a diary I kept as part of a PhD thesis over a five year period while teaching at St Matthew's. In it I noted incidents and conversations I took part in with colleagues and children, along with my thoughts on these conversations or events, and my developing thinking on race and difference. As a class teacher, it was not easy to keep a record of all the things that happened in the classroom. I found that the easiest way to do it was to jot down in a notepad or any scrap of paper the gist of conversations as soon as they happened, including exact words where a particularly significant phrase had been used. I would then add more detail at the next available break, and write up the incident and my thoughts on it in full that evening.

This way of collecting information has obvious practical advantages for teachers who want to learn more about their own teaching: keeping a diary is a well-understood process, and is both manage-able and unobtrusive. But it also has other strengths. In the chaotic day to day world of the classroom, and the too-short evenings spent marking, planning or just relaxing, there was little time or space in which to reflect upon what I was doing, and why. Keeping a diary enabled me to slow time down. By writing about a key incident in my day I was able to capture it on the page, so that I could run it back through my mind at any time, and think again about my reactions, and those of the children; to rehearse different responses and to think about what I could do next. Re-reading chains of diary entries was a way for me to look for patterns in my own and the children's behaviour over long periods of time. Events that appeared unimportant considered in isolation achieved a new significance when compared or added to earlier events recorded in the diary (Clandinin and Connelly, 2000). Keeping the diary for several years also enabled me to keep a record of the changes in my attitudes over time.

Brown and Jones (2001) suggest that one of the most powerful features of writing and re-reading diary entries is that it enables teachers to gain a degree of distance from their own thinking and behaviour, so that they can understand, analyse and ultimately begin to change it. In other words, the diary enabled me to gain a sense of control over my own teaching, and to consciously change some of my attitudes.

It is not surprising, then, that the use of diaries as a way of research-ing one's own practice is becoming increasingly common in teach-ing and other walks of life (e.g. Holly, 1989; Renck Jalongo and Isenberg, 1995). But concerns have been raised about the risks asso-ciated with researching yourself. In the first place, some argue that there is a danger that the emphasis on personal experience will mean that important social and political issues will be ignored. If we see events around us only in terms of the impact they have on us as individuals, we are not only in danger of becoming rather inward looking and narcissistic but also of misunderstanding important elements of human experience (Troyna, 1998). Some suggest that autobiographical studies are more to do with individual empower-ment than making a contribution to our understanding of how society works or how progress can be made (Hernandez Sheets, 2000). Researching oneself can undoubtedly be a powerful tool for both personal and professional development. It may be undertaken as a means of confession, therapy or personal emancipation (Convery, 1996), each of which is a good enough reason for profes-sional or personal study, but no guarantee of generating work that is relevant to a wider audience.

Thus a balance must be found between the personal and the social. Bullough and Pinnegar (2001) suggest that one way of maintaining such a balance is to see studies of the self as standing at the inter-section between biography and history. In other words, autobiographical research must make clear links between the personal and the social aspects of human experience. Neither is sufficient on its own. Social critique without personal involvement may lead to a denial of individual agency. Personal involvement without social critique may result in self absorption and narcissism. Research into one's own teaching which is meant for a wider audience must be a social endeavour. So I have tried to achieve a balance in this book between the personal and the social. I talk at length about my own personal experience but not as a confessional or as therapy, nor even for my own professional development, though I have certainly gained from this endeavour. The point of telling the story of my own development as a teacher in a multi-ethnic school is to try to under-stand better the issues that arise when teachers, and especially white teachers, deal with race and difference in the classroom. It was written to improve my own understanding but also to help other teachers and student teachers to consider aspects of their own attitudes they may not have given sufficient attention to before.

Alongside the diary, which includes conversations with children and teachers, I also spoke at length to nine of my colleagues about their experiences and views. Of the nine, all of whom were women, seven were white and English, one from an Indian and one from a West African background. While my main interest was in finding out how other white teachers understood race and difference in our multi-ethnic school, I was keen to compare their ideas with those of colleagues from non-white backgrounds. Even in the early stages I understood that race does not define us, and I knew there would be a good deal of common ground, as well as some illuminating dif-ferences between the teachers of different ethnic groups.

The importance of time and place

I began teaching at St Matthew's in the mid 1990s, a time of tran-sition in antiracist and multicultural education in the UK. The 1980s had been an era of intense debate about approaches to ethnic diversity in schools, and the issue had been high on the political and educational agenda (e.g. Jeffcoate, 1986; Sarup 1991). In contrast, in the 1990s, moves toward greater centralisation and accountability forced teachers to focus on teaching a National Curriculum and achieving high scores in national tests, so that debates about antiracism and multiculturalism were sidelined, and ethnic diversity was largely ignored (Gillborn, 2001; Jones, 1999). It was in this era that the diary was written.

Had I written it five years earlier or later, the story may well have been different. In recent years a number of national and international events have forced race back on to the public, political and educational agenda. The murder of the black teenager Stephen Lawrence in London, and the subsequent inadequate enquiry by the police; the 'war on terrorism'; increasing Islamophobia, and hostility toward asylum seekers, all point to the changing nature but continuous presence of racism. There has been a significant, though not overwhelming, response to these problems in official circles. Both the Macpherson Report (1999) into the handling of the murder of Stephen Lawrence, and the Crick Report (1998), which recommended that citizenship sessions be introduced to schools, pointed to the crucial role of schools in tackling issues of racism and inequality. That view was endorsed by the Race Relations (Amendment) Act of 2000, which places a general duty on public bodies to promote race equality.

Yet evidence persists that many schools, far from challenging racism, actually reproduce it through a range of institutional and individual practices, which disadvantage certain groups of pupils (Sewell, 1997; Haque, 1999; Gillborn and Youdell, 2000). Even more worryingly, despite the legal requirement, many schools still have no clear strategy to tackle these issues (Cline *et al*, 2002).

September 11 2001 and Islamophobia

I finished writing the diary and left St Matthew's Primary School just before the events of 9/11, and before the war on Iraq. I know that these events had a strong impact on the teachers and the many Muslim children at the school, and it would have been useful to document this period. It seems that rather than having changed attitudes to difference, those events have only made pre-existing prejudices more acceptable and old simplistic understandings of culture, religion and race more visible. Though certainly the number and intensity of violent incidents, and hostile comments and newspaper headlines has hugely increased since 2001, hostility toward Muslims has been present and growing in the West for well over a decade (Fawsi El-Solh and Mabro, 1994).

Islamophobia, the term for a hatred or fear of Muslims as a group, is a relatively new term, but prejudice against Muslims is a very old phenomenon in Britain, stretching back to the Middle Ages. Islamophobia, like all forms of racism, changes over time. It has often been said that rather than talk of racism, we should refer to racisms, since racist attitudes vary so much in different times and in different contexts. In the recent past, skin colour was the commonest focus for racism. Today, what we might call cultural racism, a prejudice against people who are culturally different, is arguably more widespread and more acceptable. At the time of writing, Islamophobia has become the commonest example of this kind of cultural racism.

Islamophobia in Britain today appears to centre on three inter-related factors. First, the secular nature of mainstream society means that many people take a sceptical, not to say hostile attitude to *all* organised religion. Second, the fact that many of the asylum seekers and refugees coming to this country are Muslims makes Islam doubly suspicious and undesirable in the minds of some people. And finally, the wars in Iraq and Afghanistan and the Israeli-Palestinian conflict, in which the UK government has appeared to side against Muslims, have combined to make Muslims and non-Muslims alike feel that Islam is seen as the enemy within in this country (Commission on British Muslims and Islamophobia, 2004). Because so many of the children at St Matthew's were Muslims, these issues loom large in the pages that follow.

The structure of the book

Chapter one begins with my first year at St Matthew's and my early realisation that there was something wrong with my teaching. At first, I was content to blame the children for the problem, but later I came to see that the narrowness of the curriculum, and subtle aspects of the school's organisation sent messages to the children about what was and was not permitted. Whatever the problem was, in these early stages I was quite sure that it was not with me: on the contrary I saw myself as very definitely part of the solution. It was only when I began to record my reflections more systematically that I noticed that some of the things I did and said excluded the children's backgrounds and experiences from the classroom. As I learned more about theories of whiteness, I became increasingly aware of my own white background as an obstacle to my ability to teach the children in a relevant way.

In chapter two, I examine other aspects of my unconscious behaviour that may have a negative effect on the children, beginning with the most difficult: my tendency to avoid dealing with racism. In trying to understand why I behaved as I did I also grapple with the sense of fear and guilt that many liberal white people feel when dealing with race. The school's Inclusion Week enabled me to put some of my new thinking into practice and provoked a range of reactions in my colleagues, which forced me to think again about my focus on whiteness.

In chapter three I examine the variety of attitudes to race and racism I encountered among the children. By far the most common approach to race was the children's tendency to avoid ever mentioning it. I explore this further, concluding that while the teachers' silence on race may have supported this, it cannot be the whole explanation for it. A complex combination of colour racism and colourblindness in Islam also appeared to be factors. I reflect on the confusion many children felt in relation to ideas about race, religion and ethnicity, and on the way in which both Muslim and white children appeared to be developing their identities with almost no support from the adults around them. These new perspectives influenced my developing ideas about race and racism still further.

In chapter four I focus on a number of my colleagues and their differing points of view on issues of race and difference. I found that while many teachers shared my sense of inhibition and uncertainty, there were some who mentioned aspects of the problem I had not considered. Paula, a white working class teacher, points to the significance of her background in cutting across ethnic differences and enabling her to address issues of identity and marginalisation with her pupils. Jane and Claire challenge my thinking about the relationship between gender and Islam. And Rose is one among many who points to the injustice of blaming teachers when the heavy burden imposed by institutional and government requirements means that teachers have no time to reflect or innovate. Each of these points of view adds a new layer of complexity to the picture.

In chapter five I explore the characteristics of the most confident of these teachers. Some teachers were much more aware than others of race as a force in their own lives as well as the children's, but struck a balance between recognising this fact and exaggerating its importance. These teachers tended to be the ones who did not see themselves as different from the families they worked with, and who saw it as part of their role to influence the children's life choices. I reflect on what less confident and experienced teachers like me can learn from their example.

In the conclusion I review the changes in my thinking over the course of the five years of writing the diary, and reflect, in the light of my experience, on whiteness as the focus of my study. I conclude that we cannot dispense with whiteness yet as it still has work to do in explaining why certain norms remain unquestioned. The ultimate goal may be for these identities to become meaningless, but that is still a long way off.

1

The Teacher as the Solution

They appear to be living in two parallel worlds, one at home and one at school.

I came to St Matthew's Primary School after teaching for two years as a newly qualified teacher on the other side of the city. There I had worked in a forbidding three storey Victorian building with high windows and a desolate playground, in a neglected area which was poorly served by local amenities. The staff was demoralised and unsupportive. At St Matthew's things were very different. The school was housed in a new one storey building set among shrubs and brightly painted playground equipment. The school was about a mile from the city centre, close to a busy market and shopping area, and surrounded by Victorian terraced houses and newer council estates. The physical contrast was equalled by the difference in the atmosphere of the school. Staff bantered in the staff room, children held doors open for each other, and chatted to teachers in the corridor. There was a feeling of warmth and calm all over the school. Well over three quarters of the children came from Pakistani or Bangladeshi families. The rest were from African or African-Caribbean backgrounds, and a few from white, Indian and Vietnamese families. But when I arrived at the school, only one class teacher and three support staff were not white.

My first class was a mixed group of seven to nine year olds. Coming to the school from one in which all but two of the children were white, I found working in this environment a challenge. On my first day in the classroom I mistook a Sikh boy in the class for a girl, because he was wearing his hair in a topknot on his head. This reduced the class to waves of laughter, and caused both me and poor Kamaljit great embarrassment. But as I got used to working there, such misunderstandings became less of a problem. I quickly learned enough about the children's religious and cultural backgrounds to avoid any more serious embarrassment, and began to enjoy working in such a lively and supportive environment. My first impressions of the school were not wrong: it was a warm and welcoming place for both children and teachers. Things were going well: I was building good relationships with the children and trying to create interesting and challenging things for them to do. Yet there was something about the way I was teaching that did not feel right. It took me years – and many false starts – to work out exactly what was wrong.

The children's attitudes

One morning I was introducing some graph work to my class. I was at the board, preparing to demonstrate how to draw a bar chart, while they sat at their tables, books and rulers ready. Needing a quick example of the kinds of information the graph could show, I asked for suggestions of the types of food that might be most popular in the class.

> The first four suggestions were 'fish and chips', 'pizza', 'roast chicken' and 'sandwiches'. At this point I stopped and asked, 'is that what you always have at home? Don't you sometimes have chapattis or rice?' The response was startling: a cry of 'aah!' went up, as if to say 'oh, you mean *our* favourite food!' They then went on to list a number of Asian dishes. They appear to be living in two parallel worlds, one at home and one at school.

All but three or four of the children in my class were from South Asian backgrounds. From conversations I had overheard, and by looking at their packed lunch boxes, I was fairly sure that they did not all regularly eat fish and chips and pizza at home. Yet they had all suggested this kind of food when first asked what was the most popular. When I queried these choices and mentioned other foods, they changed tack and began to list South Asian dishes. What was going on here? At the time, as the last sentence from my diary shows, I felt that the children did not like to talk about their home lives in school. My explanation for this was that in order to cope with the two different worlds they inhabited, the children separated their school life from their home life. It seemed to me that they had one identity at home, in which they ate chapattis and spoke Urdu, and a quite different one at school, in which they ate chips and spoke English. I thought this strange and perhaps not very healthy, but at that point I had no idea what to do about it.

Another pattern of behaviour I noticed during my first year at the school was the way the children almost always used 'white' Western names for the characters in the stories they wrote. I was quite disturbed by this, and asked colleagues whether they had had the same experience. Almost all told me they were familiar with this phenomenon, and that when they asked the children about it, they were, as one teacher put it, 'flummoxed' by the question. During a conversation in the staffroom, Penny, a white teacher who taught ten and eleven year olds, gave me a typical example of the kinds of discussions that took place:

> I was doing a story plan with my class the other day, and all the possible names for the characters they suggested were traditional English names. I said, 'why don't we have a few from your culture?' Then they came up with a few, but they clearly weren't happy about it. They seemed to feel it wasn't appropriate. In the end, they chose the name Chantal.

Rose, an experienced white teacher who initially said the children in her class did not choose Western names, emailed me some time later to tell me about a conversation she had had with her class that day:

> My kids wrote a story so at the end of the session I asked one of them to read hers out. Lo and behold the main character was called Amy. Quite an animated discussion about why this name (and other similar names) was chosen:
>
> I don't know
> It's an unusual name so it's good to use in a story
> I just liked it
> These are the names we read in books at school

I asked if characters could be called Farrah, Aisha etc and they all nodded vigorously.

In the many conversations I had with colleagues about this, we never managed to get past thinking that this was a rather strange habit, which we did not encourage, and yet we did not quite know how to move beyond the initial challenge mentioned by Penny and Rose, and that I posed in relation to the fish and chips response. Reflecting on why the children did this, our usual explanation was that it was the books, films, and television the children were exposed to that made them feel this was the appropriate way to write.

A third issue I noticed very early on was that most of the children did not seem comfortable discussing race in any direct way with teachers. At first, I noted in my diary that...

> to mention words like 'race', 'colour', 'black', 'white' is considered (by the children) to be rather shocking.

Later, I realised that while the children tended to avoid all these terms, it was the word 'black' that they considered most shocking, and there was often a quiet gasp of horror around the room whenever they heard me use it. I did not ask the children why they reacted in this way, but I did ask colleagues whether they had noticed the same thing. Sue, a white teacher in her fifties, told me about an occasion when she had been reading Caribbean poems with a group of ten and eleven year olds, all from South Asian backgrounds. She had tried to explain the history of people from the Caribbean to them:

> In doing so, she said, 'that's why they have black skin', presumably meaning because they came originally from Africa. As she said this there was an intake of breath. She asked the children why they were so shocked, and they said it was 'offensive to mention' that someone was black. Sue said she had replied that it would only be offensive if you intend it to be offensive, but to refer to someone's skin colour was not in itself offensive.

We talked about where this attitude might have come from, and Penny said that a child in her class had once told her that his Dad had told him, 'if he spoke about the colour of someone's skin he would get a smack.' We mused for a time about the attitudes to race that the children encountered at home. We all appeared to share the view that some of the children had a negative attitude to skin colour, and that it was one we did not share. But we did not talk about what we might do about this.

My initial interpretation of many of the children's attitudes to skin colour was that they were attempting to be 'colourblind'. Colour-blindness can be defined as a belief that ignoring, or pretending to ignore, the colour of a person's skin, or the fact that inequalities exist between different races, is the same as being non-racist. Those who try to be colourblind define racism as highlighting unimportant differences, and therefore, the non-racist thing to do is not to notice difference. I had more than once heard children say things like 'we're all the same really', but I had never heard any adult at the school voice opinions that I saw as colourblind. As a result I assumed that they were learning these ideas not from school but from home.

The diary entries enable me to capture what I was thinking, even at the distance of several years. And that distance enables me to be more analytical about myself than I could have been at the time. In each of these explanations of the children's behaviour, I place the emphasis on *the children* as the source of the difficulties. *They* separate home and school, *they* choose to write about white people, *they* think the term black is insulting, *they* avoid mentioning skin colour. I seemed to assume that they did all of these things because of messages they were getting from home that this was the correct way to behave. While I certainly felt that as a teacher I had a responsibility to challenge these attitudes, I had no clear idea how I might go about doing so. It did not even occur to me at this stage that my teaching might be contributing to the problem.

The idea I developed in my first year at St Matthews, that it was the children's attitudes that were the key problem, was quickly challenged as I was drawn into the life of the school. The two high points of the school year were the celebrations for Christmas and for Eid-ul-Fitr, the Muslim celebration of the end of Ramadan. While there was far more emphasis on Christmas than Eid in the run up to the festivals, the format for the main day of celebration was the same, consisting of party games in the hall, a Disney-style video, and sandwiches, crisps and chocolate at decorated tables in the classrooms afterwards. Though it was clear that the two festivals were celebrated with equal energy in an attempt to demonstrate their equal importance, the fact that the Eid party was entirely Western in its style seemed wrong to me. A few other colleagues shared this view, and we suggested that the food for Eid parties should be more closely related to the food most of the children might eat at home. This was agreed at a staff meeting, and the following year pakoras and samosas were offered alongside the chocolate and cola. The children ate them, though not with the enthusiasm we had anticipated. Afterwards, some parents said that they preferred the children to eat sandwiches and crisps, as they could have pakoras at home. The small number of us who had taken up this cause were disappointed and somewhat bemused that our attempt at being more respectful of South Asian culture was not more enthusiastically received.

Later on I learned a little more about why neither the parents nor the children had been particularly moved by our multiculturalism. Pakoras and samosas have no religious significance, and many Muslims would not see them as adding anything important to an Eid celebration. Though I was surprised that my first attempt at change had apparently failed, the incident did not diminish my feeling that change was necessary. Nor did it challenge my growing suspicion that the mismatch between home and school was caused by the school's failure to acknowledge the children's cultures, not the children's unwillingness to acknowledge the culture of the school. I began to become more aware of some of the ways in which aspects of the children's identities were ignored at school.

The monocultural school
Being Bilingual

> I occasionally come across two children having a conversation in their home language. When they see me, they stop and giggle and look embarrassed. I always ask them to carry on, but they don't want to anymore.

By the time I arrived at the school, it was unusual to hear children speaking any language other than English, and when I did so, there was always a sense that it was a slightly embarrassing thing to do.

The children seemed to have picked up the message that it was not appropriate to use their home language in school. It is unlikely that any teacher had ever told them not to use Urdu in the classroom, and yet they somehow knew that English was the only acceptable language. By the time I came to write about this incident in my diary, I was no longer inclined to see behaviour of this kind as the children's problem. It seemed clear to me that the school did not value the children's bi- or multilingualism.

In my first year at the school, there were two bilingual teachers who worked with Sylheti (a dialect from Bangladesh) and Urdu speaking children, and who supported the monolingual teachers. This support usually amounted to providing them with bilingual labels to place around the classroom and to accompany new displays. It did not extend to providing training or other materials. By the time I was in my third year at the school one of the teachers had retired and the other had taken on a new role, and bilingual support was effectively withdrawn. The following incident made me reflect on the impact of this lack of acknowledgement of the children's linguistic ability:

> Today two girls who were in my class last year bounded up to me to tell me about a visit they had received from the secondary school French teacher. They said she had hardly spoken any English at all, and they had had to answer her questions *in French*. They found this very exciting, and seemed full of admiration for someone who could do such a clever thing. Sensitised by this diary, it struck me that both of these girls are already rather proficient in a foreign language: Urdu. I could not think how to make this point without dampening their enthusiasm, so I said nothing. Is it not the case that these girls did not consider themselves to be as admirable as that French teacher because they have never been taught to value their home language by The Establishment, though their families presumably see it as important?

Apart from the important point this extract makes about the status of Urdu compared with French, what is most striking about it from my perspective is how I point the finger at 'The Establishment' as responsible for this situation: an institution I seem to regard as having nothing to do with me. Nevertheless, talking to the two girls about their French visitor did force me to look hard at my own teaching. After all, they had been in my class for a whole year, and clearly I had not taught them to value their own linguistic abilities. My support for bilingualism amounted to a set of bilingual labels on common items around my classroom. Talking to the girls reminded me of a telling exchange that had taken place in my classroom some time earlier:

> I noticed that the bilingual label on my chair had fallen off, and stood holding it for a moment, wondering what to do. 'Well, we don't really need it anyway, do we?' said one of the children. He was right. I never refer to the labels; I rarely ask the children about the languages they speak, or incorporate this knowledge into lessons; or offer opportunities for them to speak any language other than English.

I talked to Elizabeth about the changing status of bilingualism at the school. She was a white teacher in her forties, who had been working at St Matthew's for about ten years:

> It had a higher priority. It seems odd – that's completely gone – no, not completely, but... When I first came, it was clear that it was absolutely the thing to make children feel comfortable using their home language – to encourage them to do so. Now other things have become more important in the educational establishment.

Elizabeth shared my view that the reason we teachers did not support the children's bilingualism was because of pressure from above, from government and from the local education authority. Because of the pressure to perform well in the national tests, the emphasis now was on a rapid acquisition of English at the expense of other languages. This meant that, rather than seeing Sylheti- or Urdu-speaking children as possessing additional skills, they were seen as not possessing the more valuable skill of full competence in English. This attitude is clear in the following extract from an Ofsted inspection report on St Matthew's at around the time I was writing about the girls and their French experience:

> Attainment on entry to the nursery is well below what is expected from children of this age. The greatest problem is the large number of children who have little or no English when they enter the school. This restricts their development in all areas of the curriculum.

The characterisation as a problem of the children's developing ability to speak two or more languages reveals the belief that monolingualism would better prepare the children for school. Though in the 1980s and early 1990s St Matthew's, supported by the Local Education Authority, had attempted to provide a multilingual environment, by the time I arrived at the school the focus on English alone was becoming strong. Some teachers felt, as I did, that this was because of pressure to perform according to national norms in the tests. Others wondered whether it might not be natural process. Twenty years earlier most children had come to the school speaking only Urdu or Sylheti, making bilingual teaching a necessity. Now more children were starting in the nursery with at least some English, so that it was possible to ignore their other languages. This may have been part of the explanation, though given the comment of the Ofsted inspectors above, it appears that the levels of English in the children starting at school had not changed much.

The National Curriculum

My view that the school was not supporting the children's identities because of pressure to conform to government requirements was strengthened when I began to look at the curriculum with a newly critical eye. The following short but telling conversation with my class took place during the introduction to a new history topic, the Anglo Saxons. I was interrupted in mid-flow by a question from Lily, a pupil from a Bangladeshi background:

> Lily: Were the Anglo Saxons Muslims, Miss?
> SP: No, some were Christians, some were pagans
> Another pupil: Where were the Muslims, then?
> SP: Well...actually Mohammed was born at roughly the same time as the Anglo Saxons started arriving in Britain, but he lived in what is now Saudi Arabia, so he was quite a long way away. Now, we must get back to what I was talking about. The Anglo Saxons built their houses out of what is known as wattle and daub...

My immediate response to this incident was that the curriculum I was being asked to teach was inappropriate for the children I was teaching. All but two or three of the children were from Pakistani, Bengali or African-Caribbean backgrounds, and yet I was teaching them about the arrival of Anglo-Saxons into Britain, the precursors of the (white) English. It seems that I saw the role of the teacher as a transmitter of culture from generation to generation. I believed in history as a way of understanding who we are and how we got here. Apparently it had not occurred to me before, but the discussion of Anglo-Saxons, with their white-as-English connotations, made me realise that I was transmitting to my pupils a culture that was not theirs in the sense I had become used to in the mainly white school I had taught at before. It seemed that rather than enabling these children to understand who they were and where they came from, I was transmitting a clear message of exclusion.

Until this moment I had believed in my role as a transmitter of culture. I saw it as an enabling role: I was giving children the tools they needed to operate effectively in this society. But after this conversation, I began to suspect that my role as deliverer of the National Curriculum was in fact conservative, even oppressive. How were the children, whose parents came from Bangladesh or Pakistan, or whose grandparents came from Jamaica, to understand their place in the world through a study of how Anglo Saxons built their homes in 7th century England?

At the time I felt that it was inappropriate to teach *these* children about the Anglo Saxons at all. I no longer think that. Taken to its logical conclusion this means that children should only learn the history that involved their own ancestors. Clearly all children will lose out if this is the case. History can enable children to take a broader perspective, to understand how the world fits together, how relationships between countries have evolved over time. The Anglo Saxon period can be interesting and relevant to all children living in Britain, but the way I was teaching it at that time, as our collective history, was unhelpful, as Lily made abundantly clear. It took me a long time to realise that it was possible to talk about the Anglo Saxons in a much more inclusive and relevant way. The topic can be used, for example, to illustrate the diverse make up of Britain, or as an example of mass migration – making comparisons with other more recent examples from different times and parts of the world, including the migrations to and from Britain that occurred from the 1950s.

Before this exchange, my attitude to the National Curriculum may be described as resigned acceptance. As a student in the 1980s I had been well aware of the ideological nature of the choices that had guided what was included and excluded in the new National Curriculum, overseen by the ultra-conservative government of the time. But as a new teacher struggling with my workload, I was grateful for the structure it gave. I did not have to think about what I was going to teach: it was laid out for me. In the pressured environment of the primary classroom, I did not reflect much, as I once had, on *why* I was teaching what I was teaching: I concentrated on the *how.*

Lily's question jolted me out of this rather mechanistic attitude to the National Curriculum. I began to realise that I did not have to teach exactly what was written in the curriculum documents. I could instead, if I had the time and energy, provide more relevant material and still meet the requirements. I began to read more about Islam and global history in general, in the hope of being able to broaden the scope of my teaching.

Analysing my position from a distance of some years, my re-definition of the problem as to do with the Eurocentric curriculum and an emphasis on English in school seems to be much nearer the mark than my earlier focus on the children. But I still placed the emphasis on factors other than my own personal involvement. I was still the solution to a problem not of my making. It was the school, under pressure from the government, that was to blame. The curriculum I was expected to teach, and the resources I was provided with, prevented me from teaching in a more inclusive way. I was clear that that was not my fault. Nevertheless, in order to solve this problem, I saw that I would need to make some changes to my teaching. The first was to use materials that reflected a wider range of cultures and ethnicities than those I had been using. This seemed at first to be a manageable goal.

The second change was far more personally challenging. Thinking over the conversation with Lily about the Anglo Saxons, I realised that exchanges like that were rare in my classroom. Though I felt I had a good relationship with the children and prided myself on being a relaxed and approachable figure at the school, they seldom seemed to ask questions which were of importance to their lives.

More often they appeared engaged in the game of 'give the teacher what she wants', just as they had done when I asked the question about favourite foods. And as I reflected on my teaching, I began to see that I seldom asked them questions that required them to talk about home or about their own thoughts and feelings. I did not ask them to make connections between their own experience and what they were learning, as Lily had done.

So my second resolution was to find ways to draw on my own and the children's lives and experiences to stimulate their writing and talk, in an attempt to make the curriculum more relevant to them. This, combined with my efforts to use resources and lesson ideas that drew in a wider range of cultures, marked a major change in my practice as a teacher, and stimulated an enormous amount of talk. Earlier I had thought that the children made a choice to keep home and school separate. Now I saw that in fact the school and I both unconsciously transmitted the message that they were required to do so. When I began to use material that explicitly asked them to draw on their own experience, I learned a great deal more about how they made sense of many aspects of their lives. I did not anticipate then that I would learn even more about my own personal understanding of race and difference.

Invisible whiteness

By this time I had changed roles in school and was now working as a part-time support teacher, teaching small groups of children who had been identified as needing focused support. One of my groups was working on independent writing, and I had decided to use a series of pictures as a starting point for story writing. The first picture I chose was of a white boy lying on what was clearly a classroom floor. The group, which was made up of four South Asian children and one mixed heritage child, immediately named the boy Tom, and then created a story in which his arch rival was a boy named Robert. I wrote about the lesson in my diary that night:

> Though the photo required a Western name, it reminded me of the way the mostly Asian and black children in the school invariably choose such names for their characters. On the other hand, what was I doing providing a photo of a white boy, if I'm so concerned about this phenomenon? 'Oh, it was the only one I had'. And so it goes on...

Thanks to this incident I was finally able to acknowledge that the choices I as an individual made had a direct impact on what my pupils did. Until this point, I had regarded the children's habit of using Western names and faces as a consequence of the diet of images they saw on TV. But here, even though I was becoming more aware of the importance of teaching materials, I had used a picture of a white child with a group of South Asian and mixed heritage children, and then seemed surprised when they gave him a white name. In my diary I ask myself why I had chosen this photo, and my answer reveals one of the problems. Teachers have to draw on cultural resources every day in the course of their teaching, because they have to place learning in a context. They provide pictures and stories as a stimulus; they use examples and anecdotes which are inevitably and naturally drawn from their own experience. And that experience always takes place within a particular culture.

It took me a long time to realise that my own monocultural up-bringing meant that the limited cultural repertoire I could draw on in the classroom was just as problematic as the Eurocentric curriculum. Although I had identified a problem with the curriculum, and with the children writing stories as if they were white, I offered them white faces and then criticised them when they created white characters. I slowly began to see that it was being offered this constant diet of white characters and white names across the curriculum that was giving children the message that both history and fiction are about white people. In the children's experience – the experience that I and other teachers had given them – characters in books do not have Muslim names, so naturally they did not give them Muslim names in their own stories.

Though the National Curriculum certainly did not promote a multicultural approach to classroom materials, it did not actually prevent such an approach. Perhaps a less visible but far more significant obstacle in the way of a more inclusive education was the monocultural life experience of the majority of teachers in Britain's schools. I now took it for granted that many of the children tried to be colourblind, in ignoring or avoiding the question of skin colour. But now I realised that my own attitude was also a kind of colourblindness and that it had exactly the same effect. It drove home the message that we do not talk about difference: we all pretend to be the same. And being the same, in a white majority country, means all being white.

A short while later I used a different photo with the same group. This time the picture was of an informally posed group of men in graduation dress. The men were black, and were standing in the sun, smiling against a blurred background, which looked like some kind of greenery.

I recorded the response of the group, who were from Pakistani or, in Lee's case, mixed black and white backgrounds:

> Lee said, 'oh, it's the Zulus' and laughed as I put it up. They all placed the men as being from Jamaica at first, and then decided on Africa. I asked if the photo might have been taken here, and they said, 'no', and when I asked why, said, 'because they're black'. There then followed a discussion about why some people are black.
>
> The only two comments I managed to get down verbatim were:
>
> 'My uncle says people are black because they drink too much coffee and then go out in the sun'
>
> 'People are black because they haven't got enough to eat.'

There is a good deal to consider here in terms of the children's attitudes to being black. But more important for me at this stage was my involvement, or lack of it, in the conversation. I intervened to challenge the last comment, and there was fairly quickly a general agreement that it was untrue. But in my diary that evening my focus was again on the children's attitudes rather than my own:

> I was surprised, perhaps naively so, by the lack of sophistication of these children's views. I discussed it with a friend of mine, and told him that such ideas would not have surprised me coming from children somewhere like my overwhelmingly white home town, but I assumed children surrounded by different cultures would have developed a more sophisticated approach.

Discussing this incident with my friend forced me to look at it from an entirely different and more uncomfortable angle. He was not surprised that the children had confused and irrational ideas, but he did question why I had allowed a conversation about why some people are black without also asking why some people are white. It

dawned on me that in not even seeing the potential for this conversation, I had unwittingly reinforced the idea that having white skin is normal and does not need to be explained, while having black skin is the deviation from that norm and does require explanation.

White as the norm

The idea that white is the norm has a long history, one that is tied up with the European history of colonialism, which accustomed Europeans to being the viewer and the judge of what they encountered, and not to expect to be viewed and judged in return (Said, 1978; Young, 2004). We all judge what we see according to our own values and experiences, but those who do not belong to the dominant culture tend to be more aware of this process. They may have a perspective derived from family, religion or culture, but they must place it alongside one they adopt from the majority culture. Already at the age of eight, Lily, the girl who asked whether Anglo Saxons were Muslims, was becoming aware of the existence of another kind of history in addition to the one that was being presented to her by her teacher, for example.

While this kind of double vision can cause immense pain and confusion, it becomes abundantly clear to the learner that there is more than one way of looking at things. A parallel may be drawn with the fact that the knowledge that there is more than one way to say things affords multilingual people greater flexibility with both language and ideas. White people living in majority white societies can grow up without this ability to see from more than one cultural point of view and can feel that they are just people, who don't have a particular perspective. The idea that we are the norm makes white ethnic identities invisible to whites, an idea which in turn makes it possible to claim to speak for everyone. Thus for many years, in social research for example, it was possible to talk about the experiences of white women as if they were representative of all women, and in literary criticism to talk about a novel's treatment of humanity when it concerned only humans of European descent (Dyer, 1997).

The eminent black scholar W.E.B. DuBois (see DuBois, 1998) may have been the first to challenge this way of thinking in the 1920s, but it is a challenge that has been taken up with increasing frequency in recent years. *Everyone* has an ethnicity, since we all have language, traditions, ways of identifying with others who are like us and not like us. Yet the idea that white people are part of one or other ethnic group is not part of our commonsense understanding. References to ethnic jewellery, for example, may imply bangles from Africa or Asia, but not Europe. Ethnic restaurants are those that serve Indian or Lebanese food, not bistros or diners. In common parlance, ethnic means something to do with minority groups. This language gets in the way of our understanding that white people's habits, preferences and attitudes derive from their ethnic and cultural traditions in exactly the same way as other groups' do. Living in a largely white society, many white people struggle, as I did and do, even to identify those habits and preferences. We take them for granted as normal and therefore virtually invisible.

A distinction must be made between white as a racial group, defined as a group merely on the basis of skin colour, and white as an umbrella term for a whole range of ethnic and cultural groups. White people from Northern Europe, for example, cannot be said to share all the habits and attitudes of white Mexicans just because they are white. And even within one country a vast range of different lifestyles and beliefs can be found. So when I suggest that white people need to be more aware of their ethnicity, I am not saying there is only one white ethnicity. But when we complain that a child is too tired for school because they go to a mosque school in the evening, or when we express disapproval of arranged marriages, we are speaking from a particular cultural standpoint – and we should be aware of that. This is not always the same as saying we should change our views. But we should understand that the view that mosque schools are unimportant or might even be impeding learning may come from having a secular Northern European background, and the idea that arranged marriages are wrong may derive from an adherence to a cultural tradition in which romantic love is held in high regard.

When we adjust to the idea of white as an umbrella term that encompasses people as different as Greeks, Finns, Scots, Mexicans and Australians, we can begin to see what a strange idea white as a racial term is. And yet it is important that we do not let it go, because to some extent all the white people in these places may have a particular experience of life simply because they are racially white. This is so normal to many white people that it is something we are largely unaware of. We need to make an effort to see how our daily lives are affected by the ways in which our societies are structured for the convenience of the majority group and the detriment of those who are not part of it.

One source of this information is the non-white commentators who for centuries have been observing and commenting on the behaviour of white people. But such knowledge was unofficial and often unwritten (hooks, 1992). Peggy McIntosh (1992, p. 73) may have been the first white person to attempt the process of cataloguing – quite literally – what effect being white has. She cites 46 ways in which she is likely to be treated better than those who are not white. Among them she lists,

> the ability to arrange to be in the company of my own race most of the time

> being fairly sure my neighbours and strangers will be at least neutral or possibly pleasant to me

> being sure my children will be accepted at school

> never being asked to speak for all the people of my racial group

> being able to criticise my government without being seen as a cultural outsider

> being able to ignore other cultures and races without penalty

> being able to swear, wear secondhand clothes, and not answer letters without people attributing this behaviour to the bad morals, poverty or illiteracy of my race

Reading the work of McIntosh and others made me see that my life experience was structured by the fact that I was white. That race was a significant part of my life. And I began, like McIntosh, to try to track the ways in which my own attitudes were shaped in part by my whiteness.

2
The Teacher as the Problem

I didn't know what to say. Should I have challenged him? How?

Until this point I had been using my diary as a way to record what the children did and said, in order to understand them better, but in fact much of what I had learned turned out to be about myself. I had become aware that my ethnic background, my white Englishness, shaped the way I saw the world in ways that I had not previously considered, and that this lack of awareness was getting in the way of my ability to teach. But I still did not really understand how this happened and therefore had only the vaguest ideas about how to change. What was it that was I doing or saying to children – or perhaps *not* doing and saying – that caused the problem? I now began to use the diary as a way of discovering my own unconscious thinking. First I focused on an aspect of my behaviour I was already aware of: my tendency to avoid, or fail to pursue, difficult and sensitive issues in the classroom.

Avoiding difference

I used my collection of photographs again during a one to one session aimed at extending vocabulary with Hamad, an eight year old boy who spoke English as an additional language:

> There was a photo of a young girl in South Asian dress holding a baby, and I asked Hamad to describe what he could see. After

offering a sentence or two he ran out of ideas, so I prompted with:
SP: What's she wearing?
H: [hesitates] I could tell you but you wouldn't understand,
SP: Go on, I bet I would
H: A shalwar kameez
SP: Yes, I think she is

No further comment.

Why does Hamad think that I would not know what a shalwar kameez was? Simply because it's to do with his culture, which is self-evidently not mine? Because it is in a different language? It seems to reveal so much about his assumptions about the gulf between us: 'You are a white person, you don't know anything about my culture'.

I was surprised that Hamad had assumed I would not know the correct name for an item of clothing many of the children wore to school every day. It was not the first time a child had made the assumption that I would know nothing about their religion or culture. But perhaps more telling still is my reaction to Hamad's words. Though I had chosen to use these photographs as a way to stimulate discussions about cultural difference, when an opportunity to explore a common assumption among the children arose, I did not pursue the conversation. I could have asked him why he thought I would not know what he meant, but I did not. Why? I think I believed at the time that I would prove him wrong by accepting the term without comment. But perhaps I was also afraid of stirring up controversy. Perhaps I had envisaged the kind of conversation we might have being about babies in his family or the clothes his sister wore. I was not ready for the far more challenging question of the lack of understanding between him and me, between white teachers and Asian children. In retrospect I see that we would both have learned a lot more if I had confronted him, but I could not bring myself to do so.

As well as supporting individuals and groups, part of my new role was to teach the class of a senior member of staff one day per week so that she could attend to her other duties. That same term, I took a history lesson with her class of ten and eleven year olds. We were looking at accounts of evacuees' experiences in the Second World

War, one of which concerned the antisemitism encountered by two Jewish girls in an English village.

> The class was agreed this was 'nasty', 'horrible', 'mean,' and one person suggested it was racist. I agreed. Adrienne [an African-Caribbean girl] said, 'I thought you could only be racist about a person's colour.' I said I thought this was another kind of racism, which she accepted, with a mystified nod. Hamida [a Pakistani girl] still looked confused. 'Why did they do it?' she asked. 'Some people don't like people who are different do they?' I replied, a little flustered. 'So', said Hamida, 'you know I am Pakistani and you are English?' 'Yes,' I agreed. 'Does that mean you don't like me?' 'No of course not!' I said, aghast, 'but some people do feel that way, don't they?' I think I expected a general debate, but no one volunteered anything, and only Hamida and Adrienne seemed to want to continue. Unaware, or unwilling to discuss it with me?

In this brief conversation, Adrienne learned that racism is not only a matter of skin colour, and Hamida appeared to confront the idea of racism for the first time. Both girls were doing some important learning, making links between key historical events and their own experiences, and yet I did not encourage and extend them any further. I seemed to have decided that as the rest of the group was not responding, it would be wrong of me to continue the discussion. I felt that it was inappropriate for me to push the children if they did not want to pursue certain topics. I now feel there are times when this is precisely the teacher's role. I already had ample reason to suppose that they did not want to discuss the matter because they had picked up subtle messages that the issue of race is to be avoided. I wanted to challenge this way of thinking. How could I do so without asking the questions and pressing for answers?

The same faint-heartedness can be seen in another exchange with a group of eight and nine year olds after an Easter assembly which told the story of the crucifixion. Unlike most assemblies at St Matthew's, which were of a general moral nature, this one was presented in the form of a church service, attended by the local vicar who read a final prayer. I was struck by the incongruity of the overtly Christian performance for an overwhelmingly Muslim audience, and I asked the children how they felt about it as we were settling down for a small group session immediately afterwards. All the children in the group were Muslims:

SP: What did you think of the assembly?
Complete silence. The children exchanged (wary?) looks with each other but did not say anything. I let the silence continue for a few seconds, and then prompted
SP: Nothing to say at all?
Fahima: I liked the chocolate egg!
There followed an enthusiastic (and relieved?) discussion about the merits of Easter eggs
SP: What else?
Adil: I didn't like the cross (murmurs of agreement from one or two others in the group)
SP: Why?
Someone: I've never seen it before
SP (to the group): Why don't you like the cross?
Sharoze: It's not our religion.
SP: Does that mean you shouldn't talk about it?
Several children: No
Then somehow we got back to chocolate. And then to the lesson.

It was clear that the children had been uncomfortable in that assembly, and I sensed that they felt it was wrong for them to have taken part in it. From conversations I had had with him I knew that the headteacher's intention had been simply to give the children an experience of Christianity, with no thought of conversion. Yet I felt that they saw the assembly as ignoring their own faith while forcing them to acknowledge Christianity. Consequently the event was likely to be counterproductive. Rather than supporting the children in their developing faith and enabling them to understand its place alongside other faiths in their community, this assembly may have fostered a hostile approach to Christianity among some of the children.

Here again I did not pursue the conversation to a point where the children might have been able to reach an understanding of what had just happened. I left important questions unasked. Looking at these three examples, a pattern emerges in which I initiate or plan for quite significant conversations, but then fail to carry them through to the point at which real learning can occur. At the planning stage my antiracist credentials were all there, but when it comes to putting my beliefs into action, I did not quite have the nerve.

Avoiding racism

One of the most difficult things to face up to as I re-read my diary was my attitude to racism when it emerged in the classroom. The recurring theme is fear and uncertainty. One morning I was reading an extract from an autobiography with a group of nine and ten year olds. It told the story of a woman who emigrated to Britain from Jamaica in the 1950s. In the extract I had chosen, the author talked about her experiences of racist name calling in the playground. The group was a particularly confident and articulate one, in which all the children were from African-Caribbean or South Asian backgrounds. They immediately began to talk about their own experiences of racism:

> What was most striking was the number of stories the children had about racist incidents – Paul had many stories of violent confrontations. He dreamed of living in the US where it's a 'loving country'. Their shared view of Britain as a place where you have to be careful – some people won't accept you. Also moved and shaken by the lack of inhibition with which they spoke about it. The sense that this is very much a live issue for them – it's all around them. They had so much to say.

Despite working for several years in a multi-ethnic community, as a white woman I had rarely been aware of overt racism. The children talked of a world in which they were surrounded by it. This conversation brought home to me the way being white had shaped how I saw racism. That I had not been a victim of it was not surprising, but that I had rarely seen it might have been. But after school each evening I cycled away from their relatively neglected inner city multi-ethnic community and into my relatively comfortable suburban mainly white one. The notion of racial segregation was a new dimension of the problem. Thinking about it, I realised that almost all the white teachers travelled in to work from more affluent parts of the city. Just as I could move in and out of the community St Matthew's served when I wanted to I could address race when I wanted to and ignore it when I didn't. Dealing with race was optional for me but not for these children.

Another aspect of this conversation that struck me forcibly was the children's openness in discussing and trying to understand their experiences, in direct contrast to my own feelings of fear and inhibition. I also had to reflect on my approach to teaching just a couple of years earlier, when I had felt that the children were reluctant to talk about their home lives and the things which really mattered to them. This intensity and urgency now seemed to be waiting just below the surface ready to emerge at the slightest signal.

My inhibition was even harder to acknowledge and analyse in relation to my response to racist incidents in the classroom. I only occasionally heard the children make overtly racist remarks but the records I kept of these incidents show an ambivalence which revealed a good deal about my concept at the time of what counted as racism. In my diary I recounted two incidents in which Din, a nine year old Vietnamese boy, had been referred to as having 'slanty eyes':

> Afzal, a Pakistani boy, called Din 'slanty eyes, and 'flat face', reducing him to tears. I remember an incident in which Adrienne referred to his eyes as 'slanty' some time ago. On that occasion he cried too, and I did nothing more than have a 'serious talk' with the group. On that occasion, it seemed clear that no offence had been intended (does it matter?). But here it seemed obvious that the intent was malicious.

The earlier incident had occurred during a session in which the children had been asked to describe each other. Adrienne had described her friend Din's eyes as slanty, and had been horrified to find that she had offended him. It had seemed clear to me from her reaction to Din's tears that she was not, in her mind, making a racist remark. But my parenthetic question, 'does it matter?' reveals my own questioning of the offending child's point-of-view as the appropriate place from which to start. Din clearly saw the remark as offensive, and that is the more significant point-of-view. Later, I reveal again a tendency to excuse apparently racist incidents in conversation with a white colleague, Maggie, about the nature of young children's racism:

> She said that small children had sometimes used racist names but she didn't feel they were being deliberately racist. I asked whether she thought they used it as a way of retaliating when they were upset about something else, and she agreed this was probably true.

There is certainly evidence that children who do not hold racist views do sometimes use racist insults. But what is revealing about my attitude at this time is the idea that 'deliberate racism' is the key issue. Other conversations with colleagues revealed similar attitudes. When I asked if they had witnessed any racism in school, several replied that they had not seen anything they regarded as 'blatantly', 'really' or 'specifically' racist. Their use of these qualifying terms suggests that they also saw a difference between intentional and unintentional acts. There is no doubt that there is a difference. But there is a problem with seeing unthinking racist insults and unintentional stereotypical racial references as having nothing to do with racism.

What counts as racism?

Those who have little experience of it often find it difficult to understand the subtle ways in which racism works. Research in Canada and Britain has found that among white student teachers the commonest view is that racism is an individual matter, a personal failing, rather than a social problem (Levine-Rasky 2000; Gaine, 2001). Yet theorists moved away from this view of racism as early as the 1960s, focusing on processes and structures instead of individual actions and beliefs (Blauner, 1994). For if racism is only a personal matter, then racism only exists where individuals hold racist beliefs, and people can only be said to act in a racist manner if they intended to do so. And yet racism is far more widespread than this. Racism understood as a personal flaw cannot explain the continuing inequality ethnic minority groups face in, for example, employment and education, unless we are willing to believe that thousands of employers and teachers are overtly racist. This is clearly not the case.

In order to explain how and why some groups face disadvantage, broader and more complex definitions of racism have come into play. In Britain, these ideas only became part of mainstream political debate with the publication of the Macpherson Report into the murder of the black teenager Stephen Lawrence, and the subsequent handling of the case by the Metropolitan Police Service in London (Macpherson, 1999). The report brought to public attention for perhaps the first time the problem of institutional racism.

What provoked the most debate in the media was the little under-stood notion that racism had nothing to do with intentionality. Macpherson's focus on unwitting racism highlighted the impor-tance of institutional structures and processes rather than indivi-dual intention:

> Unwitting racism can arise because of lack of understanding, ig-norance or mistaken beliefs. It can arise from well intentioned but patronising words or actions. It can arise from unfamiliarity with the behaviour or cultural traditions of people or families from minority ethnic communities. It can arise from racist stereotyping of black people as potential criminals or troublemakers. Often this arises out of uncritical self-understanding born out of an inflexible police ethos of the 'traditional' way of doing things. (Macpherson, 1999, p22)

The report was careful to make it clear that in pointing to the problem of institutional racism within the Metropolitan Police Service, it was not implying that all police officers held racist beliefs. There is a huge difference between actively seeking to exclude or disadvantage certain groups, and unthinkingly applying the rules and going along with the social conventions of the organisation of which one is part. Nevertheless such rules and social conventions do sometimes exclude or make life uncomfortable for some groups. Common examples include certain dress codes, placing a higher value on speakers of European languages than those from the Indian sub-continent, or holding meetings at the pub and assum-ing everyone will want to drink alcohol. In the school context, examples might include telling a South Asian child off for using their fingers to eat, or expressing amazement when a child tells you they have eight brothers and sisters. The use of a knife and fork, and the small family are no more or less than European or Northern European norms.

As well as focusing on the significance of unconscious acts, Macpherson pointed to the fact that the consequences of certain processes are much more important than the intentions behind them. It is possible to see me struggling with this notion through the incidents in which Afzal and Adrienne comment on Din's dif-ference. I saw Afzal's actions as a clear example of racism but I was less willing to see either Adrienne's actions or those of the young children Maggie was talking about in the same light. It is not that they should be regarded as the same, it is that they are all examples of racist processes, regardless of the intention behind the remarks. Adrienne was unwittingly tapping into what must have been painfully familiar negative racial stereotypes to describe her friend. Maggie's children were copying the habit of older children and adults around them of using insults to attack their opponents, often not understanding the significance of what they were doing. And because we live in a racist society, the most wounding insults they could find were often to do with race. Whether the children *meant* to disparage their victims racially is a factor, but it is not as significant as what their use of these terms says about their developing attitudes, nor whether the victims experienced the attack as racial. The key concern is what the effect will have been on Din of hearing his physical features, his Vietnamese heritage, his difference from the other children, brought up over and over again – whether as a matter of curiosity or of ridicule. And the consequences for Din's sense of himself that his teachers did little or nothing about it.

And yet even when I did perceive racism to be deliberate, there were occasions when I still did not challenge it. For some time I continued to believe that racism was an individual problem. One morning I was reading with a boy who was in the early stages of learning English as an additional language. The incident occurred at a point where two black characters are introduced into a story about a white family. Amir, who had come from Bangladesh about a year and a half before this incident, looked at the picture in the book, and pointed to the black characters:

> Amir: I don't like them
> SP: Why not?
> Amir: I like him, and him and her and her (pointing to the white characters), but I don't like them
> SP: Why not, Amir?
> Amir: Their hair...it's (he touched his hair with his fingers, in a spiral motion) I don't like it.
> I did not know what to say. Should I have challenged him? How?

My final comments reveal my insecurity about whether and how to challenge racism in the classroom. As a result of this insecurity, I allowed Amir to make his racist remark without challenging it, and thus I colluded with him. I am still ashamed of my handling of this incident, and struggled for a long time to understand why I did nothing in the face of such obvious racist thinking. It is useful to imagine what it was about this particular incident that made me feel I did not *have* to act. I am sure I would have said something if there had been other children – and especially black children – there. So perhaps one factor in my decision not to act was that we were alone and there was no immediate victim to protect. But if this is so, it suggests that I still perceive racism as an individual matter. My words to Amir might have been along the lines of: 'we don't make racist remarks because it's hurtful to do so', which implies that if there is no obvious victim then it is acceptable to hold racist views. But in dealing with racist incidents, supporting the victim is only half of the equation. Teachers must also challenge the racist thinking that has come to light through the remarks made.

Another aspect of this incident needs considering: is it possible that I was less inclined to act because the person making the remark was himself from an ethnic minority group? Did I believe that only white on black attacks are *real* racism? This is an approach that was common in Britain in the 1980s, when the definition of racism as prejudice plus power was often invoked (Gillborn, 2001). This formula admits that any group may have prejudices about other groups, but because white people form the dominant group in the West, and hold most of the power, only whites can truly be racist. This approach brings with it a number of problems. An exclusive white-on-black definition implies that all white people are likely to be racist and all non-white people are incapable of racist thinking. In the school context, white students will not understand that because of the theoretical assumption that any white person is innately more powerful than any black person, their school's antiracist policy is in place to protect people against *them*, and not to protect everyone against racists. If antiracism is to work, it needs to gain the support of everyone. That means acknowledging that anyone can be the victim of racism, while remaining aware that in practice black and Asian people are far more likely to experience racism than white people (Clancy *et al*, 2001) and that institutional racism is a largely white problem.

I have often regretted my handling of my conversation with Amir, but clearly I was trying to challenge him. My repeated question, 'why not, Amir?' suggests that I was trying to find out the cause of his feelings. This in itself is an important aspect of racism. The notion exists that racism is an individual matter, and this is paired with the idea that it is some sort of false consciousness, an illogical perspective that is passed on from individual to individual. Yet this is not always the case: in some instances, racism works as an explanation for the situations in which people find themselves. We have to try to understand the origins of people's racism in order to find the most effective way of challenging their views (Cohen, 1992).

When I told my white colleague, Paula about my conversation with Amir she expressed the dilemma experienced by many white teachers:

> The difficulty is do you make something of a racist incident – does that make it worse? Or if not are you brushing it under the carpet?

The idea that by tackling a racist incident one could make it worse is a attitude common among many white people. Because they are less aware of the pervasiveness of racism, they feel that if it is ignored, it will simply go away. This is part of the colourblind argument that it is better to pretend not to notice difference. But Paula may be right in making the point that handling racist incidents badly can actually make the problem worse. Demonising children for racist remarks or behaviour can be counterproductive, preventing open and challenging discussion, and pushing such ideas underground where they can no longer be seen and dealt with effectively.

By now I was beginning to feel very conscious of my inadequacy in the face of racism, and felt rather low about it. I blamed myself for the lack of effective response to Amir and others, and I felt frustrated that I did not seem to be making much progress in applying my new ideas in the classroom. I felt I was thinking better, but still not acting better. There is a difficult balance to be struck between personal responsibility and an understanding of the significance of wider social influences. To see a teacher's lack of response to a racist remark as due solely to their personal inadequacy is both to underestimate the power of racism, and to place an intolerable burden on individuals. On the other hand, to argue that a teacher ignores racism in the classroom because they are part of a racialised society is to deny the power of the individual to challenge existing norms.

Those working with white student teachers on understanding the effect that being white has on their perceptions have found that focusing on individual responsibility for racism leads to a number of counterproductive reactions (Gaine, 2001; King, 2001). Some feel guilty for being white, while many others resent the implication that they should feel this way. Faced with such emotions, the result is likely to be either the inability or unwillingness to act. An alternative response is to take up a new white ethnic identity, Italian, for example, or Polish, in order to disassociate from the racism of the past. But this can lead to an attempt to claim a shared experience of discrimination with other racialised groups, and a denial of any privilege that being white affords (Levine-Rasky, 2000).

So a way must be found of thinking about race, whereby individual whites are *implicated* in but not seen as the *cause* of white domination. Rather than making white people feel guilty or resentful about being white, it may be more productive to examine what these responses can tell us about the effect race has on white people. Levine-Rasky (2000) calls this the 'double bind': white individuals feel they will be condemned if they act, and condemned if they do nothing. As a white person, to become involved in questions of race is to risk being seen as patronising or interfering, or even being labelled racist. To remain silent is to selfishly ignore the fate of others in pursuit of unearned privileges. It's a no-win situation. And that situation is caused by the fact that white people have always placed themselves outside relations of race. Because of the legacy of imperialism and slavery, and because they have no experience of racism as it manifests itself today, even those who wish to speak out on race issues feel they have no right, no credibility to do so.

There is a slightly different way of understanding my dilemma, which may be more constructive than focusing on my whiteness as the source of the problem. Frankenberg's (1993) study in the USA identified three approaches to race as expressed by a group of white women. They were racism, colourblindness (which she calls colour and power evasiveness) and colour and power cognisance. She describes how these approaches evolved one after the other over the past two hundred years, but are now all in circulation at the same time. For many years, and well into the twentieth century, race referred to a series of essential, biological differences between groups of people. These differences justified a hierarchy of races, with whites at the top. During the middle of the century, the only way to resist such racism seemed to many people to be to reject difference as the key focus, and assert the basic similarity of all peoples. Because being highly aware of race was equated with racism, it followed that ignoring race would be the way to be non-racist. The argument put forward was: 'unlike racists, we don't judge people on the basis of the colour of their skin'. Colourblindness was always intended to be a non-racist approach, but if naming difference is avoided, it is difficult to tackle the problems that persist. Ignoring them has not made them go away.

This framework explains my dilemma as being the difficulty caused by my conscious effort to change my attitude to race. I was trying to move away from colourblindness and to adopt a more colour and power cognisant stance. But a colourblind approach seeks to ignore or play down racial differences, and this makes the idea of challenging racism uncomfortable and easy to avoid. I found myself stuck between these two opposing philosophies, unsure how to act.

When I initially asked myself why I repeatedly avoided dealing effectively with racist incidents, even though I knew that in doing so I was colluding with racism, in each of my answers I saw myself acting alone. Perhaps I was simply a coward; I did not want to have to make a fuss and become unpopular with some of the children. Perhaps I felt that the most effective approach was to ignore it. Or perhaps I did not really think it was important enough: it was just someone being unkind, no different to calling someone 'four eyes' or 'fatty'. In each of these plausible explanations I saw myself as individually responsible: there was some flaw in my personality which prevented me from facing up to controversy.

This feeling that I had no right to get involved with discussions about race and racism was evident to me after a lesson I had planned on immigration and emigration in Britain in the 1950s and 60s. The day before the lesson I learned that I would be joined in the classroom by a new supply teacher, Kadeja, a Muslim woman with a Pakistani background. I recorded in my diary my worries that I had not had a chance to talk through the lesson with her beforehand, and my self-consciousness about her role and my own:

> What is this, liberal white guilt, or is it OK to think that there is something odd about a white woman talking about migration while a Pakistani woman stands by?

After the lesson I recorded:

> The children were quite interested in the texts, and I tried to highlight the main issues, which were that people were invited to come to Britain, and the racism they encountered. The children...did not seem inclined to discuss it, and I did not press very hard for them to do so. Why? Because Kadeja was there. I was afraid of saying the wrong thing. After the lesson we had a chat and were both content to blame the children for the lack of discussion...it was very friendly, and yet I had not been able to say what was on my mind. Had she?

My insecurity during this whole episode is obvious. I felt it was somehow wrong for me to be tackling these ideas while Kadeja merely helped. And yet I could not bring myself to mention my worries, or even ask her opinion about my plans, for fear of inviting some sort of challenge to my credibility. It seems to me now that I felt in the wrong because I believe it should have been Kadeja rather than me who took the lead in a lesson about immigration. Although I knew nothing about her personal experiences I wanted to impose the role of expert upon her, simply on the basis of her ethnicity. In addition to allowing white people to feel they have no role in conversations about race, this way of thinking also forces ethnic minority people into the impossible and unasked for role of expert on racism and spokesperson for all ethnic minorities.

As I came to understand some of my behaviour and attitudes better, I began to see that focusing on myself acting as an individual was counterproductive. It left me feeling guilty and inadequate and did not help me change my behaviour. It was also unhelpful to understanding my situation. Far more useful than chastising my own weakness, cowardice or selfishness is analysing the broader picture. Race is what Omi and Winant (1986) call a social fact. I am placed in a particular position in society partly because my culture and my ethnicity is given a high status. Those who have skin of a different colour or different cultures or languages are often placed in a lower position. The difference between us has little or nothing to do with biology, and nothing at all to do with innate worth. Yet the effects are no less real for that, in the realities of education, health, income, housing and so on. I did not create this situation, yet I benefit from it. And in coming to understand this, I felt the effects of living in a racialised society for the first time. In Frankenberg's terms, I was learning how race and power combine; about power cognisance.

As a white person I had not been accustomed to seeing race as something that touched me personally. I worked with other people whom race had touched, and I tried to help, but until now I did not see myself as personally involved. Now I saw that I was involved. I felt that I did not have the right to get involved in discussions about race because I was white, and as a consequence I let racist incidents go unchecked. Doing or saying nothing was not neutral; it meant colluding with racism. Looked at this way, it became clear that I had to act. I saw that I had, not the *right* to get involved, but a *duty* to do so. If I did not I would be part of the problem, not part of the solution.

The afternoon I spent with Kadeja highlighted another aspect of my behaviour I was uncomfortable with. I had not felt able to open up to her about my insecurities. I felt I had to put on a front of self-confidence, though in truth I would have preferred her to take over. Amena later made me look again at this aspect of that afternoon when she pointed out that, with two exceptions, all the people I was talking to about my project were white. While not consciously excluding ethnic minority and working class staff members, the effect of focusing only on the teachers meant that most of the people I interviewed were middle class and white. She suggested I try harder to get the two other black and Asian members of the teaching staff to speak to me, and that I should also talk to the lunchtime supervisors, who were mainly working class women from a number of different ethnic and cultural backgrounds. She also offered to help me get in touch with some of the parents at the school. I had justified my talking to white people on the basis that I wanted to find out what the teachers thought. But classroom assistants, lunchtime supervisors and parents would have had valuable perspectives on the way the school worked. Why was I so reluctant to talk to these people, who would have had so much to say? I now think I was unable to bridge the distance between us because of both race and my role as a teacher. I was on much safer ground talking to middle class white people – people like me.

While I had now begun to acknowledge the power of forces outside myself to influence my actions, I still saw myself acting as an individual. I still believed I could bring about change by simply changing my own perceptions. But this belief was called into question when I began to look in more depth at a different aspect of life at St Matthews.

The place of Christianity and Islam

Most of the children at the school identified themselves as Muslim and, if asked, would have identified the teachers as Christian. Few of the teachers would have described themselves in this way, however, myself included. Yet a Christian culture and values were all around us, while Islam was rarely mentioned. The school's identical format for celebrating Christian and Muslim festivals has been discribed. At Christmas there was also a whole school production in which each class prepared a dramatic or musical piece to be performed in front of parents, and on the last day of term the staff performed a short comical piece for the children. There was no explicit reference to Islam in any aspect of the Eid celebrations at school. The dominance of Christmas over Eid in a school in which around 90 per cent of the children were Muslims seemed wrong to me, though I contributed to it. How could it be explained? Perhaps it was because, as teachers, we knew little about the traditions and meaning of Ramadan and Eid, and this meant it was difficult to involve ourselves in teaching and learning about the celebration. But there is a also sense in which some teachers felt that the culture and religion of Islam in particular was a difficult area for them to get involved in. Discussing the complexities of teaching Muslim children, Elizabeth, a white teacher in her forties, said she found it difficult to deal with some of the things they said. She recalled a young child telling her that, as a non-Muslim, she wouldn't go to heaven:

'As someone who has a Christian background I could feel my hackles rising'... She felt it was the not knowing – 'if it was other religions you'd feel able to argue it.'

Elizabeth seems to see two obstacles to a greater understanding between her and the Muslim children she teaches. She acknowledges that it is partly her own lack of knowledge that prevents her from tackling these problems as they arise, but the fact that she feels unable to engage with Muslims in particular suggests that she sees Islam as a religion that will not tolerate dissent or debate. If other colleagues shared Elizabeth's feeling, and there is some evidence to suggest that they did, it may partly account for non-Muslim teachers' reluctance to acknowledge Ramadan and Eid in the curriculum.

This explanation looks more convincing when the teachers' attitudes to the festival of Eid are compared with their approaches to Chinese New Year. During my time at St Matthew's there were only three children at the school whose families celebrated this event, yet every year Chinese New Year was observed in some small way by most classes, including my own, by for example re-telling the story of the race between the animals or making dragon puppets. It seemed to me that Chinese New Year was seen by the staff as a non-controversial cultural event, in contrast to the religious intensity of Ramadan. As teachers we were willing to engage with difference at the level of cultural customs – food, dance, folk tales – but were reluctant to do so at the more significant and complex level of religious and, in particular, Islamic identity.

There is another explanation for teachers' reluctance to get involved with Islam. Their desire to avoid the issue may stem, at least in part, from a sense that non-Muslims have no right to organise Muslim events, and that it would be inappropriate to do so. Looked at in this way, the problem becomes less an individual one and more to do with the structure in which we worked. Perhaps the problem was the lack of involvement of parents and children in the life of the school, and the fact that the ethnic composition of the staff in no way reflected the community it served. A school structure which sought to involve parents and children more fundamentally in the planning and running of events like Eid would perhaps have addressed the profound gap between the mainly white teaching staff and the mainly Muslim community they served. The employment of more teachers from the ethnic groups the school served might have had an equally profound impact.

I am not suggesting that it is the task of teachers and parents from minority groups to educate white teachers: I have already argued to the contrary. What I am suggesting is that in the process of working alongside each other, teachers from different ethnic and social groups can learn what it means to create a genuinely diverse community, in which whiteness is less dominant.

I had a taste of how such learning might come about when I worked again with Kadeja, the Muslim teacher referred to above. This time the roles were reversed and I was asked to help her to prepare her class's contribution to the Christmas concert. That year Eid and Christmas fell within two days of each other:

> What they had prepared was a presentation that juxtaposed discussions between pairs of children about what they were getting for Eid or Christmas, and how much this would cost, with information from another child about how this amount of money could be used to help third world countries. This was followed by a song about the Arabic alphabet, each letter referring to an aspect of Islam. Kadeja asked what I thought about the song – she said she had asked the head and he had said it was OK. I said I liked it, and I thought it would be fine. In truth, I saw a strong challenge in what she was doing here. It was a good piece of theatre – so what is my problem? I suppose the seriousness of the message seemed out of kilter with the rest of the school's contributions, which tend to be about fun rather than reflection. So Kadeja's piece seemed like a rebuke to me. And then the Arabic song in the middle of all the Santa stuff seemed to say very clearly – 'what about Ramadan?'

Watching Kadeja rehearse that afternoon made two things clear to me. First, the way in which Islam, a key feature of most of the children's lives, had been largely ignored struck me with new force. Second, I was forced to reconsider my own feeble attempts to tackle the problem with the Eid celebrations, which focused on having appropriate food. I saw positive change as eating pakoras at an Eid party. In contrast, Kadeja addressed the absence of Islam from the celebrations, an issue of much greater concern for many Muslims.

Kadeja was a temporary teacher so it was not possible to build the trust that comes from working side by side with a colleague on a daily basis, which might have led to many challenging and illuminating discussions. Nevertheless, this single incident had a profound effect on my attitude. And I began to see more clearly than ever the gap between the culture of the school and the cultures of the children. It was not enough to change my own ideas. There had to be changes to the school as a whole.

Inclusion Week

It was around this time that the head asked me to work on the school's approach to inclusion with two colleagues, Sue, a white woman in her fifties, and Amena, a Muslim woman in her thirties. I was excited by the prospect, because I saw the opportunity I had been hoping for to make changes to the way the school operated as an institution. The three of us began by tackling resources, all agreeing that the school did not have enough multicultural and multilingual books and pictures. The new materials on order, we set about the second aspect of our task, which was to organise an Inclusion Week. This was an event for which teachers were asked to incorporate the biographies of high achieving individuals from non-white groups into their literacy work over the course of a week. A series of assemblies was also planned, focusing on people from non-European backgrounds who had made an impact on the world. Accompanying this was a display in the entrance hall, which featured, among others, Nelson Mandela, the US civil rights activist Rosa Parks, Al-Khwarismi, an early Muslim mathematician, and children's authors Jamilla Gavin and Malorie Blackman.

The impetus for Inclusion Week came from the head, partly as a result of pressure from a small group of parents who had complained that the school ignored the cultural and religious heritage of the families it served. The head had more than once referred to the display and others like it as 'wallpaper'. For him, Inclusion Week was a political affair – an exercise in diplomacy. He felt the school already had the right ethos, and it was now a question of being seen to do the right thing. Sue, Amena and I saw things differently. For us, it was a first attempt to raise awareness of equal opportunities in the minds of staff, and to signal a corporate change of direction to pupils and parents. There was a sense of being on a mission, an attitude that may have influenced the staff's reaction to the project.

Two entries in my diary enable me to plot the response of colleagues to the idea of Inclusion Week, and also to understand something of my own thinking at this time. The first entry records a conversation I had with Claire, a newly qualified white colleague in her twenties:

> Claire said she wasn't quite clear what to do. Would it be OK to read some stories featuring ethnic minority children? I said it was more to do with forcing ourselves to find out more about people we would not normally look at, and that the children would not get to hear about... She sort of agreed, but then said that in this school, she felt for people like Warren, the only white boy in her class. 'Looking at the display in the corridor – he's got no representation, has he? He's a minority isn't he?' I said in school he was, but in the outside world he would have things very much his own way. She 'sort of' agreed, but then said, 'we already are quite inclusive, aren't we?' I said I didn't think so. I thought we should do more, know more. She kept punctuating these comments with, 'I haven't said anything wrong, have I?' and 'I know it's not very PC'. In the end I said that the idea was that we should all be asked to go and find some resources that we wouldn't ordinarily have come across, so that next time, we use those stories simply because they are good stories, not because it's Inclusion Week. The ideal, in a way, would be that Inclusion Week would not be necessary.

In this conversation I was arguing that as a staff we should use a more culturally diverse selection of curriculum materials. However, when the conversation turned to Warren, a different aspect of my thinking is revealed. Claire said that she felt for Warren, the only white boy in the class because, 'he's got no representation, has he? He's a minority isn't he?' My reply still carries with it some of the heat I initially felt in response to that remark. I was angry that in the one week when we were finally attempting to address the gap between our teaching and the children's cultural backgrounds, Claire seemed more concerned about representation for the only white boy in her class, rather than the twenty nine other children who had little representation for the rest of the year. At the time I regarded Claire's objections as entirely wrong, and though I was uneasy about the idea of a week of activities divorced from the rest of the school timetable, I felt it was the best chance for putting the problem of the monocultural nature of the curriculum on the agenda.

I was not sure exactly why Claire objected to Inclusion Week. My fear was that she was feeling defensive about a move toward a more multicultural approach in the school. On the other hand, her objections raised important concerns about how multiculturalism should be handled so that no group feels excluded. There have been several instances of white students feeling demonised, ignored and excluded by multicultural and antiracist initiatives because they are white. One teacher recorded her dilemma at managing a scheme that funded visits to a university for ethnic minority students but not white students, which compelled her to send the daughter of an Indian-born doctor on a visit, leaving several white working class students behind (England, 2003). That teacher's sense of the injustice of this situation may mirror Claire's opposition to the idea of the Inclusion Week, which also explicitly excluded all whites, privileged or otherwise. Another teacher, Raj, who did not voice any concerns but who chose to teach about the life of Helen Keller as her contribution to the week's activities, may have shared this position. In choosing a white woman, she may have been silently criticising the use of race as the sole focus for selection. Though most teachers did contribute to the week in some way, and some did so wholeheartedly, it became clear that alongside them were colleagues who felt critical, reluctant and in some cases fearful about what they had been asked to do.

The second extract from my diary highlights the fearfulness some colleagues felt, as well as my own changing attitude to multicultural education. It records my reaction to a brief conversation I had with Barbara, a white teacher in her fifties, as she was choosing which person to focus on for her class' contribution to the week of assemblies:

> Barbara was interestingly against 'being political' – wanted to avoid anyone controversial – and indeed mentioning controversial facts about the people in question. She was not sure whether to say that the Black British woman she was focusing on had been conscious of being the only black person at college.

At the time I was rather impatient with Barbara, but looking back I can now see that her attitude fitted the ethos of Inclusion Week better than mine. The rationale for the project was to present children with positive role models, to send the message that they too could achieve success. This is a common theme of multicultural education: role models from ethnic minority groups show children that it is possible to achieve regardless of your ethnic background. But there is a danger that the message role models convey is a very conservative one. If there is no acknowledgement of the barriers that prevent some groups from achieving their potential, then what we are telling children is that we all have the same chances, and all you have to do to be a success is work hard: racism is not a factor. While the teachers who looked at the lives of Rosa Parks and Nelson Mandela could not and did not avoid talking about the racism these individuals faced, this seemed to be the dilemma Barbara was struggling with when she hesitated to discuss the fact that the woman whose story she was studying was the only black person at college. Her view of her task is that she is bringing hope to the children. She wants a positive story of hard work and perseverance leading to success. She does not want to confront them with the idea that if they are black they are less likely to succeed academically.

From a distance I can now see my reaction to Barbara's dilemma as the point at which I began to realise that the approach I had been adopting could never tackle the kind of structural racism highlighted by Barbara's chosen biography. The premise that prejudice is based on ignorance, and can therefore be dispelled when people know and understand others better, cannot answer questions about why a disproportionately small number of black students achieve success in school.

A further weakness of the approach we took, as my conversation with Claire showed, is that the exclusion of white people from the project, and the focus on individuals from non-white backgrounds, actually contributed to the very process of marginalisation Sue, Amena and I were trying to reverse. One of the dangers of isolated themed weeks or days is that they exaggerate the differences between people, as if the experiences of black, white and Asian people are entirely distinct from each other. Another is that they actually perpetuate the exclusion of some groups from the curriculum. Focusing on individuals from minority groups for one week in the year is much easier than working to incorporate a multi-ethnic dimension into all aspects of the curriculum all year round. It took me a long time to acknowledge this. Perhaps my own investment in Inclusion Week made it difficult to accept my collusion with the marginalisation process.

I had embarked on the project with high hopes that the three of us could begin to change both the resources used in the classroom and, even more significant, the way teachers thought about what they were teaching. I ended it feeling that I had made things worse rather than better. Far from giving my colleagues anything to think about, they had taught me that things were much more complex than I had first thought. As I reflected on the process, I had also to acknowledge that part of the problem was that we were compelled to operate within very tight constraints. The head, determined to keep Ofsted and the LEA at bay with reasonable test results, was not convinced that multicultural or antiracist education was necessary at St Matthew's, a school with few problems with racism, good relationships between pupils and teachers, and an ethos which supported high achievement. He saw Inclusion Week simply as a way to be seen to respond to criticisms from a few parents. The idea of one week of activities, in the last half term of the year, after the national tests, was much more manageable than a fundamental review of the curriculum, staffing, and professional development needs. Inclusion Week enabled the school to be seen to be responsive to its multi-ethnic intake while the day to day work remained largely unaffected. It was not intended to change anything.

If the sole criterion for a successful school is pupils' academic attainment, then the head was clearly right: there was no great problem at St Matthew's. But I felt the school had an additional responsibility, and that was to the children's developing identities as young British children from both minority and majority backgrounds, growing up in a multi-ethnic community and that in this they were far less successful.

3

Children's Attitudes towards Race and Identity

No one talks about colour

In my first year working at St Matthew's I believed that the children chose to keep their lives at home and school separate, and felt that it was wrong to talk about differences. Now I was convinced that they thought this was how they were supposed to behave in school and that they got this message from me, in my choice of what we learned and the things we talked about – and did not talk about – in the classroom. And they also got this message from the school as a whole, which paid little official attention to religions other than Christianity or languages other than English. I felt this must have a negative effect on their developing ideas about race and difference, and their own identities.

When I began to use teaching materials showing people from a wider range of backgrounds, I found I could learn more about the children. Photos and stories about people from different backgrounds stimulated conversations about the very things we had avoided talking about a few years earlier: religious, cultural and racial differences. One such conversation took place when I was asked to cover Rose's class of eight and nine year olds during Inclusion Week. They had been studying the life of Mary Seacole, a Jamaican nurse who had travelled to the Crimea to help tend the

soldiers during the Crimean War. The class was reading her biography in instalments, and I was asked to cover a session in which
they read that Mary's offer of help is rejected by the War Office.

> I asked the group why they thought she was rejected. Very few
> hands went up, and I asked Kofi, a boy with a Pakistani/African
> background. 'Because she was black', he said. I agreed, and we
> talked about the incident. I introduced the word 'racist' at some
> point, and someone said, 'what's that?' I explained what racism
> was, and Paul, an African-Caribbean boy, joined in, with some
> emotion in his voice, saying that he wished everyone would live in
> peace, and he was going to change things. I supported his com-
> ments, and we talked some more, but there was a strange sense of
> reserve in the group as a whole. Paul, Kofi and I were involved in
> the discussion, but the others were almost completely silent, ex-
> cept for one boy, Azim, who in the middle of the conversation put
> his hand up and said, 'Miss you're going to think this is a bit
> cheeky...' He stopped and giggled, before resuming, 'some people
> think black people are pooh'. As I tackled this, Paul looked miserable
> and hurt. Again, there was very little reaction from the other chil-
> dren to this exchange.

This conversation encapsulates the range of attitudes to race I encountered among the children at St Matthew's. The few who raised
the issue of racism were clearly aware of it as a feature of their own
lives, and felt that it was appropriate to talk about it. A couple asked
'what is racism?' as they were genuinely unfamiliar with the term.
This does not necessarily mean that they had never come across it
but it suggests that racism had not been discussed in the classroom
before. A small number of children used racist ideas and language.
But the commonest attitude to race was the one most of the children in this class adopted: they sat in total silence during this part
of the conversation, though they had responded eagerly to earlier
questions about Mary Seacole's adventures elsewhere.

As I probed their attitudes it appeared that many of the children did
not have fixed ideas about race but were constantly monitoring
each other and the teachers to see what was and was not acceptable
at any given time. Nevertheless, the pattern that emerged in the
conversation about Mary Seacole was repeated many times over in
later conversations, and I was struck by the similarity of this pattern

to the framework of the three approaches to race identified by Frankenberg (1993) and outlined in the previous chapter.

Colourblindness

I was reading the autobiography of Malorie Blackman, a black British author, with four nine year olds one morning. Only Patrick was white:

> At one point she states, 'I chose to write because I was sick of reading books with no black characters in them'. Patrick muttered something at this point, and looked aggrieved. I asked what the problem was, and he said, 'That's racist. You don't call people that.' I said I didn't think calling someone black was racist, and that the author herself was using the term. He said on The Bill (popular police drama on TV) he had heard someone 'complaining about a black person doing something, and the man he was talking to, who was... that (meaning black) had said, 'black people, black people, all you can ever talk about is black people.' I said I thought maybe the man was saying he didn't think it was right to blame black people for everything, rather than that it was wrong to use the word 'black'. Patrick looked unconvinced. During this exchange, none of the other three got involved at all.

Patrick felt strongly about this issue and seemed angry with me for what he saw as my support for what was, in his terms, an example of racism. He saw the use of the term black as inherently racist. He did not understand the message the author was trying to convey: that black people in British society are not given enough recognition. It is a view that is part of a more radical antiracist agenda, but Patrick did not understand it. In fact, the approach he adopted, followed to its logical conclusion, made it impossible for him to challenge discrimination of the sort the author was talking about, because it meant not using the language we need to talk about discrimination. You cannot point out, and then begin to address the discrimination faced by some ethnic groups if you are not allowed to mention discrimination and ethnicity. In other words, it is impossible to be both colourblind and antiracist. The way Patrick used a situation he had seen acted out on television also offered me a clue to how children make sense of the information available to them. Children often use ideas they have seen on television to support their own perception of events, even when those ideas actually have a quite different intention, as here. Taking a colourblind approach, Patrick thinks that any reference to a person being black is racist, and he uses the words of the character on The Bill to reinforce his argument. Because he understands the situation only in these terms, he is not open to the more radical message that he could have picked up from this episode.

The three other children sitting around the table – all from South Asian Muslim backgrounds – said nothing. Their silence here, and in the conversation relating to Mary Seacole, was typical of responses whenever I raised the question of race and difference. I came to see these silences as a different form of colourblindness. People who try to be colourblind feel that making an issue about the colour of people's skin is wrong. So my reference to Mary Seacole's skin colour, and my discussion with Patrick, caused them difficulty. They could not criticise me for speaking of these things because I was the teacher. But neither could they join in, because they felt the conversation should not be taking place at all. The only option, therefore, was silence. This interpretation of their attitudes is backed up by several incidents mentioned by colleagues. It was made clearer to me by the following conversation, in which a group of children did talk openly about how they felt about references to skin colour:

> Reading aloud with a group of nine year olds. The story refers to a character in the book as 'the black boy' at one point. As one of the children read these words, after a slight hesitation, there was an audible gasp around the table. I asked, 'what's the problem?'

> > Saira: 'it's nasty'
> > Shahzeb: 'it's racist'
> > Hassan: 'it'll make him sad'
> > SP: is it an insult to call someone black?
> > all except one child: 'yes'
> > Tayyiba: no – it's just your colour.

Saira and Hassan are clear that referring to someone as 'black' is inherently insulting. Shahzeb went further and suggested that to do so is actually racist. Tayyiba appeared to be expressing another theme of colourblindness: that skin colour is not important.

The children's colourblindness was one of the first things I noticed when I came to work at St Matthew's, and at first I had been content to see the school as playing no part in supporting this attitude. Later, I began to see that if we as teachers did not speak of differences of many kinds, we were implicitly teaching children that race is a forbidden subject.

Yet this was still not the whole story. I had never heard any of the African-Caribbean children at the school take a colourblind approach. It was only the few white and the many South Asian Muslim children who preferred to pretend that racial differences did not exist. Where did these ideas come from? Frankenberg's research (1993), among others, has shown that the commonest approach to race among many white people is colourblindness. But I could not at first understand why the South Asian children seemed to share this approach. There are several competing theories.

Orientation to whiteness

Research in the US found that some students of colour shared with their white counterparts what they termed an 'orientation to whiteness'. These students seemed to adopt a white perspective because it was easier psychologically than constantly setting oneself against mainstream ideas (Hunter and Nettles, 1999). It may be that young ethnic minority children living in a mainly white society and learning in a school staffed almost entirely by white teachers also sometimes adopt a white standpoint. A study conducted in Britain found that black and Asian children depicted themselves as white, because they had become used to thinking of people as *white* people (Burgess-Macey, 1992). This makes sense of the other early concern I had had about the children's tendency to use white names for characters in their stories. Perhaps, then, the mainly South Asian children at St Matthew's had taken on the attitudes of the mainly white adults around them as their own.

'Shadism'

The children's colourblindness did not amount to a simple aversion to all references to skin colour, however. Though it was rare to hear children discussing skin colour of their own accord, on those occasions when I had asked the children in my classes to draw self portraits, I was often called on to help to choose the appropriate pencil for their skin colour. This appeared to be a difficult decision for some South Asian children, though I had never tried to explore why. Elizabeth had also had experience of this kind of conversation, but in her case the children had been more open about the hierarchy of acceptable skin colours:

> One child had complained of a classmate, 'miss he says I've got brown skin and I've got white'. The child was clearly insulted. Yet some are quite happy to use a brown pencil. Others ask, 'what colour is my skin?'

This conversation suggests that the confusion over skin colour that I had noticed in my classes was also common in her class of five and six year olds. When I asked about the children who were happy to use a brown pencil for their skin, Elizabeth said this tended to be the African-Caribbean children, who were in her view 'more sorted on this issue'. The conversation also reveals a possible reason why so many children hesitated to use a brown pencil to depict themselves. The child whose comments Elizabeth remembered was obviously unhappy to be considered brown rather than white.

Though most children would, if pressed, use the terms white and brown to refer to skin colour, few would voluntarily use the term black. This word was, in their minds, only ever used as an insult. One source of this attitude is a long held association of dark skin with low-caste or class status. Kaye, a white teacher who had taught mainly in an inner London school, was familiar with the problem:

> From discussions I've had with predominantly Bengali children, the darker your skin, the more inferior you are in the Bengali community itself. To refer to someone as having black skin is highly offensive, because obviously the whiter it looks, the higher up the social scale you are.

Only two children ever spoke to me directly about this sensitive issue. During a detailed discussion with a group of ten year olds about prejudice, one girl of Bangladeshi origin said:

> Whiter skin is better than dark. If someone says I've got black skin, I don't like it.

One cannot know how widespread this attitude to skin colour was among the South Asian children at the school, though the comment of one African Muslim girl suggests it was quite common:

> She said 'the paler-skinned Pakistani children' in the reception classes stared at her sometimes when she went past. I asked why she thought they did that and she said it was because of her colour.

It is interesting that it is the youngest children in the school who stare: the ones who have not yet learned to pretend to ignore skin colour.

The influence of Islam

As a world faith which draws in believers from many cultures and nations, Islam teaches that race and ethnicity are irrelevant to Muslims. There is a strong belief in *umma*, a worldwide community of all Muslims, regardless of colour or ethnicity. The idea that racism is unislamic is common in official publications on Islam:

> Each ethnic and racial group, which embraced Islam, made its contribution to the one Islamic civilisation to which everyone belonged. The sense of brotherhood and sisterhood was so much emphasised that it overcame all local attachments to a particular tribe, race, or language – all of which became subservient to the universal brotherhood and sisterhood of Islam. (Islam Awareness Project, 2003, p4)

Such statements represent high ideals, which are worth struggling for. But as Tariq Modood (1992, p272-3) has pointed out, they are unlikely to be sufficient on their own to stop people from holding prejudices about other groups:

> The Quranic teaching is that people are to be valued in terms of virtue not colour or race. ... Like all 'colour-blind' approaches, it has two weaknesses... First, it is too weak to prevent racial and ethnic prejudice... Asians have no fewer stereotypes about whites and blacks than these groups have about Asians or about each other. The second weakness flows from the first... Some very recent Muslim position statements seem to express a reluctance for what is essential to positive action, heightening racial categories.

I never heard a child refer to Islam when explaining their reluctance to raise the question of skin colour, but children had told me that their parents had told them not to speak of it, or themselves expressed the view that 'it is offensive to mention it'. The vast majority of the children at the school were practicing Muslims, so it seems fair to suggest that Islam was influential in the children's thinking, though there was also clear evidence of a cultural prejudice against dark skin.

Racism

As I watched and listened to the children talking, I could see that they drew on any and all sources of information to help them understand the world and their place in it. They picked up on messages from Islam, the school, their families and wider society, and tried to make sense of them in their own way, and not always as intended – as with Patrick's interpretation of the episode from The Bill. This led to some revealing exchanges. On one occasion I was working on a reading comprehension exercise with a group of eight year olds. I had chosen a piece about a black woman in Britain who wanted to become a doctor. In the text she describes how, as a child, she had believed that this would not be possible, since all the doctors she had met were white. She then travelled to Africa, where she met a black woman doctor and was inspired to take up medicine. One of the comprehension questions asked, 'what important event took place in Africa?' In answer to this question, Maria, an eight year old girl from a Pakistani background, wrote:

> 'she met a black doctor, but she didn't care'. I asked her what she meant by this, genuinely unclear, and she said, 'she didn't care that she was black'.

One cannot be sure what Maria meant by this remark, but it seems likely that she sees the African doctor's skin colour as a problem about which the girl in the story can be broadminded: 'she didn't care'. Maria does not understand that the narrator herself is black and that she sees the doctor as a role model. This is an interesting example of the orientation to whiteness phenomenon. Perhaps it does not occur to Maria that the girl is black because she so rarely has access to stories featuring non-white characters. There are elements of both racism and colourblindness in Maria's words. She seems to be suggesting that to be black is to be inferior in some way, an idea at the heart of racism. On the other hand, she feels that the girl in the story does not mind the colour of the doctor's skin, an aspect of colourblindness. This is perhaps how Maria has reworked the ideas she has heard about race: to be black is to be in some way inferior, but one should try to be tolerant.

Not all incidents were as subtle. A white colleague told me about a dispute between two South Asian girls and a black girl in an infant class:

> Famida, a Pakistani girl, told Zara, a black girl, that she couldn't be (the third girl's) friend. Zara got upset, and came to (the teacher) about it. She asked why Zara couldn't be her friend. Famida told her that it was because she was not white. The teacher asked, 'like who?' confused because Famida herself wasn't white in the sense that she understood it. Famida said 'like me', as if it was obvious.

Famida's attitude seems to be an example of the dark skin prejudice discussed above. Her reference to herself as white makes this clear. This caused confusion for the teacher, for whom Famida cannot be white: for her, whiteness relates to European origins. For Famida it relates simply to the shade of her skin. This illustrates the range of racisms that exist. It seems that Famida's racism initially confused the teacher, since she was more familiar with the kind of racism which sees different cultural or religious values, rather than skin colour, as alien and threatening.

Nevertheless, explicit incidents of racism were unusual. More common were subtle incidents that revealed a negative attitude toward difference, even in this relatively diverse school population. Children who did not belong to one of the main ethnic groups in the school sometimes fell victim to ridicule or exclusion. I also occasionally heard children using racist language and ideas for their own purposes. One afternoon two ten year old boys came to me at the end of a lesson, claiming that a girl had called them names. The boys were African and Vietnamese, and the girl of mixed white and African-Caribbean background:

> I took them both outside and asked them what had happened. Christopher said that Liza had called him a crybaby, and Din had told her not to be so horrible. She had then turned to Din and made some rude comment, and pulled her eyes up and outwards to indicate 'slitty eyes'.

It became clear that the original dispute between Liza and Christopher had had nothing to do with race, and that Liza was using a racist taunt to undermine Din, because he had annoyed her by supporting Christopher. Din, it will be remembered, often had to suffer taunts about his race.

Sometimes the abuse was even subtler, but still motivated by a desire to wound. This was not necessarily racist in origin but it consciously used racism to great effect. One afternoon I was working with a group of five nine year olds, four boys and one girl. All were Muslim except one boy, Lee, who came from a mixed African-Caribbean and white background. We were working on a story called 'The Three Little Wolves and the Big Bad Pig', a reworking of the traditional story of the Three Little Pigs. During the lesson Lee kept talking to his friend instead of working, so I made him move away from his friend and sit next to Sadiyah, the only girl in the group. This seemed to work, as the group then settled to work quietly:

> Lee had decided to include everyone in the group in the story, so that his friend Hassan became the beaver, Riaz the kangaroo and so on. Sadiyah made a protest along the lines of, 'he's being rude...' I shushed her, not seeing a problem, and then, a minute or so later, after another monitoring trip round the group, read Lee's story properly. This time I saw that he had given the pig character Sadiyah's name.

Lee used his knowledge that pigs are regarded as unclean in Islam to insult someone in the group by linking her name with the pig character in his story. There is no reason to assume that he disliked Sadiyah because she was Muslim: it is more likely that he wanted to upset her simply to vent his anger at being made to sit beside her. Yet he used an aspect of her Muslim identity to achieve this.

Sometimes children used race or ethnicity as a way to exclude individuals from the group. One day I found Caitlin, a nine year old white girl who had an uneasy relationship with a group of girls from Pakistani backgrounds in her class, in the canteen eating her lunch alone while the rest of her group sat chatting nearby. Thinking she had had an argument with them, I asked her who she was playing with that day:

> Caitlin: Maria and that lot
> SP: How come you aren't sitting with them?
> Caitlin: I don't really like sitting with them.
> SP: Why not?
> Caitlin: Because I don't like sitting with them when I've got sausages
> SP: Have you got sausages today?
> Caitlin: No, but once I heard Maria and Azmina laughing at me because I had sausages.

I wish I had asked Caitlin to tell me why she thought having sausages would make Maria and Azmina laugh. But one can guess that it was because that was something they, as Muslims, would not eat, thus cementing their shared relationship at Caitlin's expense. It is difficult to be sure of the reason for Caitlin's part-time status in the group of girls led by Maria but it seemed clear that Caitlin herself felt that her difficulties stemmed from the fact that she did not share the culture of the other girls in the group.

According to the teachers, the most common form of racism at the school was a derogatory attitude toward Bangladeshi children on the part of Pakistani children. Several teachers spoke of 'a pecking order', and of Bangladeshis being seen as 'the poor relation', though longer serving members of staff noted that this was less of a problem now than in the past. The following exchange was typical. The boys were both eight:

> Looking at a picture of a pelican with a fish in its mouth:
> Faheem [Pakistani heritage]: Bengalis eat fish
> Amir [Bangladeshi, clearly irritated]: So? Everyone eats fish.
> SP: I eat fish
> Faheem: I don't. Not like them.

Again, I was troubled by the weakness of my response to Faheem's words. I had tried to support Amir, but had not really let Faheem know that his attitude was unacceptable. I do not know how other teachers dealt with situations like this, though they were all highly aware of periodic animosity between the two groups.

Recording all these subtle and less subtle forms of racism made me think again about my initial view of racism as a white on black problem, manifested in straightforward physical and verbal attacks.

It now seemed a much more complicated and intangible problem, one that could not be dealt with effectively as a teacher acting alone. There needed to be a whole school approach to difference, and a clear message from all staff about the values of the school, and what was and was not acceptable.

Colour and power cognisance

Though most of the children at the school did not talk about race and often seemed deliberately to avoid doing so, a few children had a noticeably different attitude. African-Caribbean children at the school did not share with South Asian and white children a reluctance to use the word black in reference to a person's skin:

> A group of nine children looking at a text I've used before: *The Trouble with Donovan Croft*. The excerpt I used starts at chapter five, necessitating a bit of background information. I explained that the main character, Donovan, is being fostered because his mum has had to go to Jamaica to look after her dad. 'So he's black?' asked Adrienne. 'Yes,' I replied. She gave a slight smile, and a significant look to her (African-Caribbean) friend.

Adrienne is perfectly comfortable with the term black, in marked contrast to most of her classmates. Her question about whether the character is black also suggests that Adrienne feels the character's ethnic origin is important. Again, this is in sharp contrast to the colourblind approach, which tries to see difference as unimportant. Her smile and her glance at her friend suggest that she is very familiar with questions of race.

Some children saw racism as an appropriate topic for discussion, and as an attitude that should be challenged. Zinat, a seven year old girl of Pakistani origin, was telling a literacy group about her cousin who had come to stay:

> She said a teacher had been kicked out by a headteacher at his school for saying, 'hey, Paki' to a child. I said, 'quite right too', and Zinat looked slightly belligerent, as though justice had been done.

Having read an extract from Floella Benjamin's account of the racism she experienced at school in Britain in the 1950s, a group of children aged between seven and nine reflected on their own experiences of racism:

Paul, an African-Caribbean boy, said he had a Pakistani friend who once called him 'gali'. Paul had said, 'I don't know what you mean but I don't like it – don't call me that'. And he stopped.' I said I didn't know what 'gali' meant, and Atiya explained that it means black: 'People pretend it's just describing, but really it's abusing.'

Later, Paul said that

Some people thought that black people were going to take over the country, but really they are very kind and just want to fit in.

Paul mentioned a common racist theme of black people 'taking over the country,' suggesting that he is aware that African-Caribbeans face social disadvantage as a group as well as individual prejudice. Earlier he had shown that he was able to challenge the racism he faced, and Atiya had shown a sophisticated understanding of the power of words. While the children were rarely the ones to initiate discussions about racism in the way Zinat had, when I raised the issue some children did show a keen awareness of it. However, the level of understanding of the nature of racism shown by Paul and Atiya did not seem to be widespread among the children.

Confusion and resistance: racial, national and religious identity

I was now convinced that the reason colourblindness at St Matthew's was so widespread was due to a combination of factors. First, the absence of race and difference from the curriculum and from the day to day talk of the mainly white teachers like me; second, a widespread cultural prejudice against dark skin among the South Asian children, and thirdly a colourblind approach to race equality in Islam. I felt that this silence meant that the children had no forum in which they could develop more sophisticated ways of thinking about racial, ethnic, cultural and religious difference, and in which racist ideas in circulation could be challenged. Certainly more egalitarian ideas did circulate in the school, voiced by both teachers and children, but they were rare. I wanted to know what effect this was having on the children's developing sense of their own identities.

Children develop a sense of themselves by drawing on the various ideas available to them, principally through the home, the media, and the school (Francis, 1998). Because colourblindness is so dominant in mainstream society, in school – and for many white and South Asian children also at home – the options available to the children at St Matthew's were limited. Colourblindness explicitly prevents discussion of issues crucial to the development of sophisticated and flexible ideas about identity, and so children's perceptions of themselves and others were likely to remain undeveloped and confused. It is not surprising that children of eleven and younger had unsophisticated understandings of such complex ideas as culture and nationality. What *is* surprising – and worrying – is that few attempts were made by teachers to help children develop a more nuanced approach.

Sometimes the source of the confusion was simply unfamiliarity with the vocabulary. A chance conversation with a group of ten and eleven year olds revealed their lack of understanding of a term that I had expected children of that age to be familiar with:

> Rosina was the only girl sitting on a table of boys, including two older boys visiting from the local secondary school – ex-pupils who had come to help out as they had the morning off. There was a lot of backslapping and male bonding going on, from which Rosina was clearly excluded. She asked if she could move and I said yes. Mohammed, who was sitting on the other side of the room, then asked if he could move on to that table, and I said no. I did not want the backslapping to escalate. He was annoyed, and started moaning under his breath, and Imran piped up, 'Miss, that's racist!' I turned to him in astonishment: 'how is it racist?' I asked. 'You let Rosina move, but you didn't let Mohammed!' he said. 'You may think that's unfair,' I said, 'but it's not racist, is it? What word do you mean?' I was hoping he would see he meant sexist, but he just looked confused. No one else offered any help. 'You might think it's sexist', I offered, and a few of the girls said, 'oh, yes, sexist'. Imran said, 'yeah, it's sexist'. We then had to go to assembly, and I said, 'we can discuss this later if you want to'. But of course we didn't.

Looking back on this incident, it seemed to me that Mohammed was either using the term racist as a catch-all term for unfair, or he had confused racism with sexism. The fact that the children were not used to using these terms does not mean they were unfamiliar with the ideas behind them but it does suggest that they had not discussed either subject in the classroom. Once again, it seemed to me, the children were left floundering because as teachers we did not help them to understand these difficult but important aspects of their own experience.

The most obvious manifestation of such lack of understanding was the confusion over skin colour, religion and nationality. Again, this is not surprising, since many adults share their confusion. For most of the South Asian Muslim children, all 'brown' people were Muslims, and all 'English' or white people were Christians, as the following extracts from my diary show. Each comes from group work with nine year old children:

> Faisa was talking about a boy at summer club. Joseph asked, 'was he black?' and she said no, he was white. Joseph said, 'that means he's a Christian'. Zinat glanced at me, and then turned to him and said, dismissively, 'of course'.

> A photo of a man and woman from Guatemala. One child decided they were Muslims – I asked why and he replied 'because they are brown.' but this was contested by two others, one who said that not all brown people are Muslims, and another who said you don't have to be brown to be a Muslim – white people are Muslims too. I added that black people might also be Muslim, citing another teacher, Amena, whose parents came from Nigeria. This caused some surprise – they did not appear to know that she was a Muslim, though she wears full Islamic dress.

In the first extract, Joseph, of mixed white and African-Caribbean background – who was happy to use the word black – and Zinat, a girl of Pakistani background, shared an assumption that whiteness and Christianity always go together. In the second extract the group discussed various opinions about the relationship of Islam to skin colour. Two children challenged the idea that all Muslims have brown skin. And yet none of them were aware that a black teacher at the school was a Muslim, though she wore the *hijab*. It seemed that the fact that she was black made her Muslim identity difficult for them to recognise, though the idea that white people could be Muslims was voiced. For many children, this idea, too, is difficult. Many white teachers reported conversations with South Asian Muslim children, which were almost identical to the pattern described by my colleague Kaye:

> All through my career I have tried to have this discussion about the difference between your country of origin and the religion you're brought up in or choose to follow. And the children find that so difficult to understand...[I say] 'I could be a Muslim.' [They say] 'No you can't, you're English.'

Paula told me that when some Bosnian boys had come to the school a few years before, the other children had found it hard to understand that they were Muslims, because they were white. Their mothers had started to wear shalwar kameez and scarf after a while, so that they would be recognised and accepted as Muslims.

This simplistic understanding of the relationship between skin colour, religion and nationality causes two major problems. First, the children's idea that black people or white cannot be Muslims excludes African and European Muslims from the Muslim community and is contrary to fundamental ideal of the unity in diversity of Islam. Second, assumptions about whiteness as synonymous with Englishness prevent ethnic minority groups from adopting an English or British sense of national identity. This problem came to light during a discussion with a group of nine year olds about a white teacher who had worn a sari to school at Eid:

> This caused surprise and confusion in the group. I tried to say that your nationality and your religion are not the same thing. To which Shozad responded by saying that he had seen white people at the mosque. Humza found this very surprising. We talked a bit more about nationality, and Humza listened, wide eyed, and asked 'Could I be English?' 'Could I be Christian?' I said that whether you were English depended partly on what you feel yourself. He decided he was both Pakistani and English.

Shozad, whose mother is white, is aware that white people can be Muslims, though Humza is very surprised to hear this. He also makes it clear that the idea of his being English is entirely new to him – and his questions, 'could I be English? Could I be Christian?' imply that he sees the two as amounting to the same thing. Later, though, he decides to adopt an identity that is both English (not Christian) and Pakistani. He does not mention Islam, which suggests he is beginning to understand the difference between nationality and religion. Most children shared Humza's assumption of their identity as Muslim, or, less often, Pakistani or Bangladeshi, as distinct from teachers who were 'English'. I often heard children speak of 'my language', meaning Urdu or Sylheti, implying that English was not, therefore, their language, even though these children were bilingual and often most fluent in English. It is difficult to know whether the children's understanding of their primary identity as 'not English' is a consequence of the local Muslim community's desire to maintain a strong Muslim identity, or whether it was a result of a racist assumption common in wider society that you cannot be both Muslim and English. Humza's spontaneous decision to label himself Pakistani and English suggests that the latter reason has more influence with him. Seeing for the first time that he is able to label himself English, he promptly does so, retaining his Pakistani identity alongside it. For him, the identity that fits best is a hybrid one. In a conversation about national identity, two older children showed that they had already thought about their identity quite carefully:

> Din and Taiba both expressed very strongly the idea that they felt the UK was their country. Taiba said that when she went to Pakistan she liked it, but she didn't feel that it was home – the language was different, and her friends were not there. She felt more comfortable in Britain. Din said that though it [Vietnam] was his parents' country, it was not his.

These two eleven year olds saw themselves as British, though both had earlier spoken of their experiences of racism. Din showed a sophisticated understanding of the way in which his identity differed from his parents'. Taiba was clear that adopting a British national identity did not conflict with her identity as a Muslim. Din and Taiba's confident assertions of a hybrid identity offer hope for those who want to encourage children to find ways of defining themselves that they can feel comfortable with. Nevertheless, they were in a minority.

As these conversations show, opportunities did arise for teachers to confront children's misconceptions. Kaye's story about telling children she could also be a Muslim suggests that she routinely challenged assumptions about Islam's relationship to nationality. Discussions of this kind offered excellent opportunities for more detailed and challenging exploration of what different aspects of identity meant to the children though, as I have admitted, I was one teacher who did not always take up such opportunities. More often, conversations began promisingly but were not pursued, as in this discussion with a group of nine year olds:

> Reading a piece called An Iranian Dinner. It talked about the kind of food people in Iran eat, and mentioned that they were Muslims. Some of the familiar reactions to encountering non-Indian sub-continental Muslims appeared: 'they don't look like Muslims', said Hamad, looking at the photo. 'What does a Muslim look like?' I asked. 'Brown' came the reply. 'Can you tell whether someone is a Muslim by looking at them?' I persisted. 'By what they eat' said Riaz. I said 'yes, but just by looking at them?' 'By how they speak' said someone, but in the end, they agreed you couldn't tell.

Once again the children started with an assumption that all Muslims have brown skin, but then began to suggest ways of identifying a Muslim that relate to ethnicity: food and language. This could have led to a revealing discussion about the difference between ethnicity and religion, though again I did not pursue it. I wish I had. I now feel that conversations like this can allow children to begin to develop a more sophisticated understanding of who they are by learning about concepts like culture and nationality alongside more subtle definitions of religion and colour. Becoming comfortable with these terms may help them to develop a sense of their identity which sees Britishness as compatible with different cultural – and, more importantly for Muslims, religious – identities.

Resistance and inhibition: Muslim children's identities

Taiba's description of herself as both British and Muslim was rare among the children. More common was the thinking underlying the following response to a rebuke from me:

> A literacy session – the group was sluggish, and their answers sloppy. I said, 'What has happened to your English?' Sabina said, under her breath, 'I'm a Muslim.' At the time I interpreted that remark as meaning, 'it's not my first language', and, thinking she thought I was getting at them, I said something like, 'it's nothing to do with that Sabina, your English was fine yesterday.' She didn't respond. Now I wonder if she meant, 'I'm not English, so don't expect me to be'. Or did she hear 'your English' as 'you're English' and instantly refute it?

It is not clear exactly what Sabina meant by her response, 'I'm a Muslim', but I think she used the word 'Muslim' in instant opposition to the word 'English', and that she meant 'English' as a national identity, not a language. Whatever the precise meaning of her remark, Sabina did seem to be saying, on some level, that she was *not* English. An interesting discussion might have ensued about what being English meant to Sabina, and the possibility of being both English and a Muslim. Again, I did not take the opportunity. Several other small incidents like this suggested that other Muslim children at St Matthew's saw the two identities as in conflict. In some cases this was because of the link between Englishness and Christianity. Amena, the only Muslim teacher at the school, believed that this was an insoluble problem for state schools with a large Muslim intake. She felt that the children did not listen to non-Muslim teachers on religious or moral matters:

> The children don't really think it's to do with them. They disassociate themselves from it...There's a barrier. I don't think we'll ever get the children to cross that barrier.

She told a story about her six year old daughter to illustrate her point:

> She was reading to Amena in the kitchen. It was the story of Noah's Ark, which her teacher had given her to read at home. They had been talking about it in school because of all the recent flooding. She kept getting stuck on a word, and when Amena came to look at what was causing the difficulty she found that the word was God. Amena explained that God was another word for Allah, the creator. She explained that the story of Noah was also in the Koran. After that she seemed reassured and she read the word without hesitation. Amena said she had never told her daughter to behave in this way; she had just picked it up.

Amena believed that her daughter's identity as a Muslim was developing in opposition to Christianity, which she saw as being supported by the school. Yet the story of Noah's Ark was used by her teacher simply as a way of reinforcing work in literacy on the floods we had been experiencing in the local area at that time. In other words, she used the story as a cultural rather than religious resource: she was drawing on her own cultural repertoire. In fact, the story also appears in the Koran, and it would have been very helpful if the teacher had mentioned this to the children. It would have been a good way to reinforce the shared history of the two religions and would also have contributed to a better balance in the curriculum between Christianity and other religions. Because the teacher failed to do this, Amena's daughter did not see the story in cultural or cross-cultural terms but purely as Christian.

Other children also occasionally made comments which suggested that their Muslim identity was being formed with some kind of resistance to Christianity at its heart:

> This morning Sabina was sitting on the table rather than on a chair, the better to see what was going on at the other end of the table, where I was handing out stickers. Khurram said to her, 'why are you sitting on the table, are you a Christian?' She looked bemused, and I asked what that meant. He looked embarrassed, and wouldn't answer. Everyone else said, 'he doesn't mean anything,' or looked as confused as me.

I still do not know whether this link between sitting on a table and being a Christian has any particular significance, or whether Khurram was simply using the term as an insult to a fellow Muslim. The other children in the group seemed to share my puzzlement at the outlandishness of the remark.

This was not the only time Khurram made comments which suggested he was doing a great deal of thinking and learning about his Muslim identity at this time. The following week I came across him again:

> I was in the computer room at lunchtime to gather some materials for the afternoon, and a group of children were in there for a voluntary session. Sabina said something like, 'come and help me I beg you', to one of her friends, to which Khurram responded, 'Muslims don't beg.' I asked him what he meant, but then Sabina came over to him and started to explain, as I interpret it, that she was saying, 'please, please' help, rather than asking for money.

One can do no more than guess at Khurram's thinking about his identity from these two brief remarks. He does seem to be absorbing strong messages at this time in his life about how Muslims behave, and there is some sense that his Muslim identity is developing in clear contrast to a Christian one. While Khurram was the most outspoken and unequivocal in his comments, I sometimes heard other children trying out their ideas about what it means to be a Muslim in Britain in similar ways:

> At lunchtime I was setting up a tank of frog spawn and some children gathered around to watch. Imran saw a tattoo on someone and said to another boy, 'we're not allowed to have tattoos are we?' The boy did not give a clear answer, so he asked another, who just shrugged. 'Why not?' I asked Imran. 'Because Muslims don't do that.' 'Even a temporary one?' I asked, thinking of the craze for them that many children got involved in a couple of years ago. He shrugged.

> I often hear this, 'we don't do that', 'Muslims can't do that'. Yasmin said it the other day when I was eating my hoummus: 'Muslims don't eat that', even though it was untrue in that case. Do the children learn that their identity is based on not doing or being certain things that they see all around them?

Because of my own lack of knowledge I was not in a position to help children like Khurram, Imran and Yasmin to forge an identity that they could be comfortable with: an identity was both British and Muslim. I had no guidance to offer in terms of Muslims and tattoos, nor any way of knowing whether Khurram's point about sitting on tables was based on any kind of religious teaching. And because I did not know very much, I sometimes still felt uneasy about getting involved in these conversations.

On the other hand, I was fairly confident that there was nothing in hoummus that made it haram – forbidden for Muslims – and I said so to the girls I was having lunch with. They did not seem inclined to believe me, however. Was that because I was a non-Muslim or because my argument was not convincing enough? Again, I did not pursue the conversation long enough to find out.

The on-going religious debate between Sabina and Khurram revealed more about the other children's perception of what it was and was not acceptable to talk about in school:

> As I turned to write something on the board there was a brief 'aah' from the group. Sabina explained that Khurram had said a word that he was not allowed to say, according to Islam. Khurram protested that lots of people said it, but Sabina said that they shouldn't – you weren't allowed to. Akeel added, 'until you have read the

whole of the Koran', which Sabina agreed was true. She was genuinely upset for him, and anxious to explain what he was doing wrong. Khurram, who I suspect would normally ignore anything Sabina said, being cooler and cleverer than her by most people's reckoning, was clearly listening to what she had to say, and was uneasy about his position. He even listened to Akeel, though he had been scathing towards him minutes before. Even more interesting was the reaction of Imrana, and later Akeel, who started saying, 'let's get back to work now', and 'Ms Pearce is waiting', 'look – *Ms Pearce*', meaning, I assumed, 'don't have this conversation in front of Ms Pearce. At one point I said, 'no, it's OK, it's interesting'. But then the conversation fizzled out – or did I stop it by speaking and reminding them of my presence? I sensed Imrana's relief.

Two of the children in the group seemed very uncomfortable that this conversation was taking place in front of me. They may have interpreted my silence, and the fact that I was looking at them, as signs that I was waiting for them to stop talking and be ready for the lesson. These were indeed common teacher tactics, but other conversations were not usually ended with such minimal intervention, so this is not the most likely reason for their discomfort. I felt that they thought Islam should not be discussed in the classroom. My statement, 'no, it's OK, it's interesting', did not reassure them. My intention was to let them continue the conversation, so that I could find out more about how they thought as Muslims. Yet my words may have reinforced their notion that white teachers do not have anything to do with their identity as Muslims. I did not try to get involved in the conversation, only to listen to it. Despite my intentions, I may have contributed to their assumption about the marginal position of their faith in school.

This same sense of a Muslim identity being something one could not be entirely open about in school also seemed to be shared by a six year old boy I chatted to during the infant department's Eid party:

> As I was standing beside him watching the game, he suddenly said, 'I didn't celebrate Christmas'. I said, 'oh, I see – did you celebrate Eid?' and he nodded, looking slightly worried. Claire, his teacher, heard this exchange and told me that a while ago he had come up to her and said, 'Miss, I've got a secret. I'm a Muslim.' She had said something like, 'OK that's fine,' and the conversation ended there.

The boy's first comment only seems significant alongside the earlier comment. Taken together, the two remarks suggest that he sees his Muslim identity as an unwelcome subject in the classroom and is confused about the position he should take to the two festivals. Again, though I am sure the teacher's response was intended to make him feel there was nothing to worry about, she did not help him to gain confidence in expressing his Muslim identity at school. There is no knowing how common this situation was in other class-rooms, though at interview some teachers spoke of the children's willingness to discuss Islam, and of their efforts to include references to it. And had I been asked whether I encouraged chil-dren to talk about Islam, I would have said that I did.

Confusion and resistance: white children and race

Just as some Muslim children in the school appeared to be develop-ing their identities in opposition to what they saw as the Christian values of the school and the teachers – and with very little inter-vention from them – the few white children at St Matthew's were also very much alone in their attempts to understand their identities. Each of the four white children I worked most closely with as a support teacher was involved in an incident which re-vealed their insecurity about how to behave in the multi-ethnic environment of the school. Just as misconceptions about relationships between race and religion were the source of con-fusion for the Muslim children, the white children struggled with confused ideas about what it means to be white.

Patrick was the nine year old who had objected to the use of the word black during an earlier discussion. His troubled attempts to be antiracist are again apparent in the extract below, in which he was part of a group reading the story of the bus boycott during the Civil Rights campaign in the US:

> Patrick, who has complained in the past at my use of the term black, was clearly under pressure as we read a text that contained the word about thirty times. He did not say anything this time, though. There was lots of 'why did they do this?' type discussion. I said something on the lines of, 'well, some people are racist aren't they? Why? That's a good question'. Patrick said – 'are we?' to me, mean-ing, I think, 'are we racist?'

The following day I read the same text with a different group which included Caitlin, the white girl who had difficulties with friends. The differences in their reactions to the story struck me at the time:

> The others had a lot to say, but she kept saying things like, 'can we get on with our work now?' and 'I think we should be getting on with our work now'. Clearly very uncomfortable with her role in this sort of discussion. Comparing her remarks with Patrick's it seems they are both in a difficult situation and don't know how to deal with it. And I'm falling into the classic trap, casting whites as the villains, not showing them where they can stand.

Patrick's poignant question about whether he and I, as the only white people in the group, were racist, suggested to me that he had encountered the idea that racism was a part of a white identity. I do not know whether he said this simply in response to the portrayal of whites in the bus boycott story, or whether the idea had a longer history in his mind. It was clear that he did not want to be racist, but he seemed unsure whether he would be able to escape that fate. My response to his question was naturally to explain that anyone could be racist, and that he and I were both against any type of racism. However, I am still haunted by the inadequacy of my response. Reflecting on Caitlin's reaction to the same story, I still worry that I was unable to show them how to resist racism without falling victim to the self-hatred to which Patrick in particular seemed vulnerable. Caitlin's position was less clear. While the other, Muslim, children were involved in an animated discussion about the story, which was my main objective, Caitlin kept urging them to get back to the comprehension questions, in order to close the conversation down. She was clearly uncomfortable with the issues being raised, though as she was less open about this than Patrick, it is difficult to explain exactly why. Once again, I failed to show her that she was not personally implicated in the story, and that she could choose a different identity from the racist identity adopted by the whites in the story.

Caitlin's attitude during the Civil Rights discussion was certainly very defensive, but I had worked with Caitlin for longer than most of the other children, and I had noticed that in other circumstances she was often curious about the backgrounds of the other children in her class, and conscious in particular of Islam. This may well relate to her on-off friendship with a group of Muslim girls in her class. I recorded in my diary an interesting exchange between Caitlin and Faisa, which had occurred two years earlier:

> Working with three children on writing skills today. We were discussing the recent death of the school guinea pig. Faisa, who is Muslim and Somali said the words guinea pig, and Caitlin turned to her in mild surprise and said, 'don't you have to say p-i-g?', referring to the practice of spelling out the word rather than saying it, which is sometimes heard around the school. Faisa looked puzzled, and looked to me to explain. I said, 'some people do that, but not everyone.'

At the time of this incident I had focused on Faisa's role in this conversation rather than Caitlin's, because after Caitlin pointed out the now quite unusual habit of spelling the word for pig rather than saying it, (because pigs are regarded as unclean in Islam) Faisa started doing this, though with a twinkle in her eye. But in retrospect, Caitlin was revealing a lot about her attitudes here too. She was aware of the way the Muslim children around her behaved, and particularly attuned to the things they did that were different from what she did. On another occasion, I was talking to Caitlin, Faisa and Joseph, a boy of mixed white and African-Caribbean heritage, about a girl in their class who had been away from school for some time:

> Faisa said she'd been away for weeks. Then Joseph said, 'aaahh she missed mosque this whole time!' and waved his arms around to indicate the extraordinary length of time. There was a silence while Caitlin looked at him, frowning, for a moment, then said 'do you go to mosque?' He didn't reply.

I got the impression here that Caitlin had been sure that Joseph, who was not South Asian, was not a Muslim, but then had been confused by his mention of the mosque. There were other incidents like this in which Caitlin, in particular, asked questions of other children which suggested that she was trying hard to understand the children around her, but not getting very complete information, and therefore never quite becoming comfortable with the differences that surrounded her. I wondered what effect this was having on her sense of herself and of the Muslim children she was growing up alongside, but not exactly with.

The two other white children I worked with were involved in an incident that suggested a very different reaction to racial difference. Joseph was the boy who had confused Caitlin, and who had shared with Zinat the assumption that being white meant being Christian. He had a white father and a mother of white-Caribbean heritage. On one occasion, he had turned to the others working at a table and said, out of the blue, 'I am the only one here who goes to church'. He was thus very conscious of his position as one of the few Christians in the school, and may have been unsure about his own ethnic identity. The other boy, Mark, was white, and they were both part of my literacy group of seven and eight year olds. I wrote down my reaction to the conversation just after it occurred:

> I showed them a big book on Festivals. There were one or two groans, and one or two cries of 'Muslim!' and Pakistani!' when they saw the cover, which showed two Muslim boys hugging, and the interior of a church. Joseph turned to Mark and said, quietly but not in a whisper, 'I hate this. Don't you hate this?' Mark grinned, looked embarrassed, and nodded. During the discussion, which focused on Muslim, Hindu and Christian festivals, Mark joined in with the others, but Joseph was almost completely silent.

> What did Joseph mean when he said he hated this? What did he mean by 'this'? In the past, Joseph has made it clear he is conscious of his minority status in the group, having one black grandparent and a Christian faith. On the other hand, he does not like literacy, so he could have meant that, though Mark's embarrassed reaction suggests he didn't think so. I think he meant he hated having to look at yet another book about Sikhs and Muslims, and all those other things that have nothing to do with him. Why did Mark smile, look embarrassed and nod? He knew I was looking at them. He knows it is frowned upon to express negative feelings about such things as different festivals. Or was he embarrassed by Joseph's views? He nodded, and yet he joined in with the discussion. Did he want to keep in with his friend Joseph but at the same time did not share his views? Or did he agree with Joseph, but did not want to risk getting into trouble by refusing to participate? Or did his naturally sociable character get the better of him, even though he'd have preferred me to produce a book about football or Christmas?

I could not tell whether Joseph's negative response to the book was a result of feeling excluded or defensive in the face of my attempts to use culturally diverse resources or not, but I felt that it might be, given other remarks he had made about Christianity.

This was the only example of a response of this kind from a child during the course of seven years at the school. Nevertheless, it does raise questions about how all children may be included in attempts to introduce a more inclusive curriculum. Approaches that exclude or demonise one or more groups are likely to stimulate either guilt or resentment, as the incidents with Patrick, Caitlin and Joseph show (Scottish Executive, 2001). This was the point Claire may have been making when she objected to the exclusion of white people from Inclusion Week. They leave white people with no way of articulating their sincere antiracism. Such approaches also repeat the mistakes of the past in presenting a racial group as homogeneous. Often the message received is that all whites are the same: inevitably racist. Or that white people are always the most privileged group and never experience marginalisation or abuse. Clearly, this does not match the day to day experience of many whites, and that was the point that Raj was trying to make in her choice of Helen Keller, a blind and deaf white woman, as a role model in her class.

By now I had discarded my earlier belief that the children did not want to talk about race and difference. My overwhelming feeling was that they were thinking a great deal about these questions, but that they were doing so with almost no support from the adults around them. Thus, though a few children had developed admirably sophisticated and confident ideas about who they were, most were confused, inhibited and defensive and sometimes mildly hostile. In the middle of a multi-ethnic city, these children were growing up with very little idea about how to be black, or white, or Muslim, and British.

4

Teachers' Views on
Race and Difference

I couldn't be sure it wasn't a religious issue. I don't know, do I?

For some time, my project was intensely personal. Though I was open with my colleagues about what I was doing, and had useful conversations with them about the dilemmas I was struggling with, particularly as a result of Inclusion Week, I generally worked alone. Possibly I needed this time to work through my prejudices and inhibitions in private, but after a time it became clear that I needed to open up more to my colleagues if what I was doing was to make any difference and also help me make sense of my experiences. Talking to the teachers at greater length was like opening a window. I found many colleagues who shared my fears and inhibitions, others who had struggled with the same dilemmas and found a way through them, and a third group who were just beginning to try to grapple with the situation they found themselves in. I found colleagues who agreed with me and those who had different perspectives. All the teachers I spoke to were concerned, as I was, that there was a mismatch between the curriculum and the backgrounds of the children in their classes. But few agreed wholeheartedly with my view that the solution to the problem was within us as individual teachers: that it was our monocultural backgrounds that caused the difficulties. Their differing perspectives forced me to think again.

'Saying the wrong thing'

A few colleagues admitted to sharing my early sense of insecurity on questions of race and difference, variously describing situations in which they had felt uncertain about how to act appropriately as 'a minefield', 'getting into deep water', and worries over 'saying the wrong thing' – unintentionally saying something that might be construed as racist. Elizabeth, a white teacher in her forties, talked about her insecurity about saying Pakistan was the home country of many of the pupils:

> Am I being racist when I say that? I feel as though I am saying the wrong thing when some of the children have never been to Pakistan, for example.

Elizabeth found it difficult to find a way of talking about and to the children that recognised their identities as both Pakistani and British. She wanted to acknowledge their Pakistani heritage and the fact that many still had strong ties to Pakistan. But she did not want to appear to treat the children as if they were not British. Several other teachers spoke of their worry that they would be considered racist when attempting to tackle questions like this. The logical approach for some was to avoid them all together. In the last chapter, I highlighted colourblindness as the commonest approach to race among the children, and noted that I never heard a teacher speak in the same terms. I spoke about pupils' silence as a form of colourblindness, and perhaps the teachers' avoidance of questions of race was another form of it.

Colourblindness

Frankenberg (1993) suggests that colour and power evasiveness is a more accurate way to describe an approach to race which both seeks to avoid mention of racial difference *and* refuses to confront the fact that inequalities arise from it. Often the two evasions go hand in hand, but in the case of some teachers at St Matthew's, it was power evasiveness and not colour evasiveness that caused difficulties. Most teachers were quite comfortable with acknowledging the racial and cultural differences they saw around them, but far fewer were happy to confront the possibility of a power imbalance that was a direct consequence of those racial or ethnic differences. Barbara's worry about telling the children about a black woman who reported that she was the only black person in her college is a good example. She had no difficulty highlighting the significance of this aspiring doctor being black, but she did find it hard to tell the children that being black meant that she was less likely to go to college. Barbara's dilemma highlights the key problem with power evasiveness: if you behave as though racial and ethnic differences have no effect on life chances, you suggest there is a level playing field. That in turn suggests that any failure is the fault of the individual and downplays the significance of wider social forces.

Race and ethnicity in Initial Teacher Education

Just as tight constraints on the curriculum at St Matthew's were felt to have squeezed multiculturalism out, so the amount of time spent on issues of race in initial teacher training courses has dwindled as education departments struggle to meet curriculum-centred official requirements in the limited time available (Jones, 1999). This was certainly true of my own training in the early 1990s. I wondered whether this was the experience of teachers who had trained at other times, so I asked my colleagues what they remembered of their training on matters of race and ethnicity.

Not one replied that they felt their training prepared them well for dealing with issues of race and difference in the classroom. I was not alone: teachers who trained in the 1960s, 1980s and mid 1990s all reported that they had received at best one or two lectures on the subject. The best for Paula was an RE course which proved useful for factual information and 'not to make a *faux pas*'. Rose, who trained in a mainly white area in the 1960s, spent one day in a multi-ethnic school in Birmingham. Trained at about the same time, Jane received no input on bilingualism and minority cultures, and found this surprising and frustrating, as she then did a teaching practice with a class of Asian children newly arrived in Britain. The two Newly Qualified Teachers (NQT), Raj and Claire, told similar stories. Raj talked about a memorable lecture that was conducted entirely in Russian, to give them the sense of what it was like for children with no English, and a session on using books which refer to more than one culture. Claire's training did not offer even one lecture on the subject:

> On the first day we got a pack on Equal Opportunities, but we were overwhelmed by paper, and within three days we'd been asked to write two essays so, to be honest, I didn't really look at it. It was never explained or gone through.' There were one or two lectures on SEN which mentioned EAL children. On her second teaching practice she had two EAL children, and had some help from a woman who was in charge of EAL.

Though the teachers tended to feel that such paltry input on issues they then encountered was inappropriate, many also felt, as Raj put it, that the best approach was, 'learning on the job, learning what works'.

'Learning on the job' suggests that Raj sees teaching as a craft, an activity in which one develops practical skills. This view of teaching is common, as implied in the term 'teacher *training*'. Teachers seemed to see their courses as helping them to acquire a series of practical skills which they could take straight into the classroom. They seldom saw themselves as involved in teacher *education*, which is concerned with more fundamental and less tangible changes in attitudes and values (Elliott, 1993). Thus, Claire, having volunteered to learn Urdu in her own time during her training, ended the course feeling it had been a waste of time:

> I thought, 'how much help is it going to be to anyone that I can speak (badly) a few words of Urdu?'

If Claire's goal was to be able to communicate fluently with parents and children with limited English, then clearly she had a point. But this goal is directed, as mine was at the beginning of this project, at her capacity to help the children over their lack of English. She is the solution to a problem outside herself. But the usefulness of the course can be assessed in a different way: it can be seen as enabling monolingual teachers to recognise that their monolingual background and lack of knowledge of other cultures could be an obstacle for them, and that as committed teachers they should do something about it. Looked at like this, the problem resides with the monocultural teacher, not the child. And the change that is sought is not competence in another language but a shift in attitude.

Later, Claire remembered some relevant inservice training (INSET) she had attended, and her comments again suggest that she is looking for straightforward tips and activity ideas: she sees no need to critically reflect on her own attitudes:

> Lots of interesting points had been raised, 'lots of food for thought'. It was mainly about confidence and identity for children who were in a minority in school, which wasn't as relevant here. And most of the ideas were good, but totally impractical – 'there was nothing I could use in class the next day, no user-friendly solutions'.

My first reaction to these words was disappointment. As if diversity were something that could be addressed with a well-designed worksheet. But re-reading Claire's words, I realised that I was overlooking a key aspect of Claire's work. As a new teacher, she was working extremely hard to keep up with the relentless pace the National Curriculum required, working in an unfamiliar environment with few resources and little experience. Of course she wanted user-friendly solutions: there was no time for anything else.

The National Curriculum

My colleagues often cited the National Curriculum as the greatest obstacle to planning more inclusive, relevant work with the children. Since the early 1990s, the National Curriculum had laid down quite narrow requirements about what should be taught in primary schools. At the time of its inception, fierce debates had raged in the media about the appropriateness of the curriculum for a multi-ethnic society. Indeed, it was widely understood to have been developed specifically to protect and support a narrow white, male and middle class view of British culture (Gillborn, 1996; Blair and Cole, 2000; Hill, 2001). A decade and several amendments later, many of the teachers were still unhappy with the curriculum. Jane, a white teacher in her fifties, felt the history curriculum in particular was, 'very, very Eurocentric'. Kaye expressed her frustration at the changes she had been forced to make in her multi-ethnic school in inner London when the National Curriculum was introduced:

> I was horrified when it first came out... it was so ethnocentric... 'we're all wonderful, all white' – especially history and geography.' She said they had been looking at Bangladesh, and then they had to stop and look at the Romans instead – 'or, if you're doing World

War II, 'ask your grandparents how it was!'... it's not their history. In the first year you get really pissed off with it. But gradually you accept it as a *fait accompli* and get on with it.

Kaye's resigned attitude after her initial anger echoes my own principled objection to the curriculum while studying at university and how it faded to compliance when I began to teach. The introduction of the Literacy Strategy, which gives teachers even less control over what they teach and how, has exacerbated the situation for many teachers: Kaye said that her previous school had maintained a genuinely multicultural curriculum throughout the early years of the National Curriculum, but the situation at St Matthew's in the late 1990s was very different:

Everything is so structured. Unless the literacy strategy says use a book from a different culture, you don't.

Paula, who in principle supported the introduction of the National Curriculum as an entitlement, also expressed misgivings:

It gives a baseline on what everyone else is doing. In the '70s, the attitude was, 'these Asian kids can't cope', but most of these kids are second generation now, they should be doing it. I think elements of it could be... a bit more appreciative of where they're coming from, and going to.

When I raised the question of why, as teachers, we did not adapt the curriculum to make it more relevant to the children's experiences, Rose promptly replied:

Time, resources, and lack of knowledge. If you don't know you can't include it.

Several teachers admitted that they made no attempt to innovate because they felt they did not know enough. Elizabeth commented:

There is a lack of knowledge. Helen [a reception teacher colleague] was telling me about the time she had introduced Islamic patters in art, expecting the children to be somewhat familiar with the designs, but they had apparently never seen anything like it. We are often acting on false information. And we are also afraid of saying the wrong thing.

Claire, the newly qualified white teacher, told me:

> I once used a book with a picture of a Rajah on the cover. The children laughed at it. I was amazed at the reaction. I thought it would be culturally familiar, and then wondered, 'why should it be familiar when they were born and brought up in England?'

These comments highlight two problems. First they indicate teachers' lack of knowledge about the pupils' home lives. The assumption that the children would be familiar with Islamic art and images of Indian rulers suggests a notion of the lives of South Asian Muslims that is drawn from books rather than from living and working alongside people from the Pakistani and Bangladeshi communities in the North of England. Helen took as her starting point the pictures with the geometric patterns on the ceilings and walls in mosques in Islamabad or Baghdad, perhaps. But the children's experience of a mosque is more likely to be the converted church hall or semi-detached house down the road. Claire's comment reveals her growing awareness of the problem, but as a newly qualified teacher from a monocultural background, she seems to be learning through a process of trial and error rather than any explicit training or induction by more experienced and knowledgeable colleagues. Helen had been a teacher at the school for many years, and was still unsure how to relate to the children's cultural backgrounds.

Paula, on the other hand, was well aware of the bicultural identities of the children, but she encountered the same problems as Helen over classroom material to reflect that reality:

> The trouble is the books we do have tend to be about people in Pakistan or Africa, and what is needed is something about Asian kids in Britain, not Pakistan, but living with the two cultures.

The second concern raised by the comments of Elizabeth and Claire is the nature of the knowledge teachers felt they lacked. These teachers said they needed factual knowledge about the cultural backgrounds of the children, not that they wanted to gain greater understanding of issues like institutional racism, and the nature of culture and difference. They emphasise cross-cultural approaches to learning. Only two teachers mentioned antiracism as a necessary element of the curriculum. Amena felt strongly that racism should be addressed at an early age. With her knowledge of the National

Curriculum at key stages 3 and 4 because of her own teenage children, she observed:

> At secondary school the children learn a lot, but I wonder whether it might be better to learn about atrocities early rather than later – the anger some youths feel when they learn these things can make them go haywire.

My journal records an occasion when Rose asked to have a copy of the material I had prepared for a lesson on racism. Her comment reflects her acknowledgement that racism should be tackled in school and points again to the difficulties of finding good material:

> It would be good to have more meaty things on hand to use. The problem was that when you are busy you just reach for what's there, which is not necessarily anything very challenging, and so you never deal with these things.

While a significant number of the teachers I spoke to frankly admitted that one of the reasons they did not adapt the curriculum was that they did not know enough, they were unanimous in their view that the key problem posed by the National Curriculum was the lack of time it left for other aspects of children's learning. The pressures of trying to deliver the curriculum – a phrase many teachers took issue with – left no time during the school day to discuss social and personal matters with the children. Rose talked about a book on Martin Luther King which she had used as a text for the literacy hour, and how this had led to a class discussion about the civil rights movement:

> The children really wanted answers. It was really interesting. The trouble is there isn't always the time...Things arise out of the most unlikely things. It's having the time to deal with it.

Elizabeth and Claire both felt this pressure exerted by the curriculum. Working with very young children, they were concerned that they knew so little about their home lives:

> Elizabeth: The way the curriculum is going, there are fewer opportunities to discuss this with children.
> Claire: I would like more social time with the children. Then I could find out more.
> Elizabeth: But when do you do it? It's so pressured. There are no opportunities.

Conversations like these revealed the impact the National Curriculum had on teachers' ability to teach to their own satisfaction. They reminded me of my own early focus on the difficulties posed by working with a narrow and structured curriculum. Significantly, in my new role as a support teacher, I worked mostly with small groups on maths and literacy based lessons, and thus the pressure I felt so strongly in the first few years of my career had lessened considerably. The teachers who were still working full time and teaching the whole curriculum in challenging classrooms provided a timely reminder of the reality for most teachers. Living with the constant pressure to deliver a centrally agreed curriculum, which I had partially escaped, gave them a different perspective.

I was therefore forced to reconsider why I persisted in planning for but not following through conversations with the children about race and difference. I had first seen these incidents as examples of my lack of courage in pursuing difficult or controversial conversations and later as symptomatic of the bystander role being white pushed me into. In contrast, the full time teachers saw the main problem not in terms of wanting to avoid controversy or race but of time constraints imposed by the National Curriculum. They read my habit of stopping these conversations as due to my obligation to return to what they called my script, the official and conventional material I had prepared for the session that I should stick to. How could I allow the whole lesson to be taken up by an interesting but, in terms of curriculum coverage, ultimately irrelevant discussion? They recognised this as a common feature of their own teaching lives. Rose described herself as feeling 'hamstrung' at times, and Jane said that she often felt 'straitjacketed' by the pressure to stay with her script:

> I often have to say, 'well we can't really go down that road now,' but when this happens to me I always feel cross and think, 'well, why not?' Because I'd like to, I would like to sort of open it up. Because the questions they are asking me are often more interesting than the questions I'm asking them.

This consciousness of there being a script which teachers are required to stick to in the classroom is a relatively new phenomenon but it is one which, with the advent of the National Curriculum, many teachers recognised. Education had increasingly come to be seen as the rather uncomplicated transfer of an officially regulated body of knowledge rather than an interactive, dynamic process requiring the emotional and intellectual involvement of both teacher and pupil.

Such discussions led me to rethink my reasons for shutting down conversations with the children, and I began to feel that my colleagues were right. While my consciousness of my insufficient knowledge and my inhibitions about subjects such as race may have been a factor, I had not paid enough attention to other influences which prevented me from pursuing a more child-centred and thus more inclusive agenda. On re-reading my diary, I found the following entry, which seemed to illustrate the unconscious process of coming to accept the notion of teaching and learning as the transfer of knowledge rather than something more personally involving. In it, I compare the importance of the more inclusive approach I was beginning to adopt as part of my research with the requirements of the National Curriculum:

> I have been assigned to a group that has been less forthcoming about the issues I am interested in than the others. My fault, I suppose: I concentrated on the others, and almost excluded this group from my study. It's a group of children who came up to the junior department unable to read, and I think I thought, 'right, with this group I'll just teach, and forget the complicated stuff – I can't afford to mess about with them'. Which misses the point a bit. What I did with the other groups was simply bring in opportunities for them to talk about home, or religion, and I can do that with this group too.

The phrase, 'I'll just teach, and forget the complicated stuff' reveals my characterisation of social and personal matters as optional extras, interesting and beneficial, but not fundamental to the learning of young children. What is fundamental is their ability to read. In this entry I see teaching as the transmission of knowledge, not a social, creative process. I characterised the situation then as a dilemma between my priorities as a teacher and as a researcher. As a teacher I saw it as my duty to equip them with the basic skills they needed; as a researcher I wanted to find out their opinions. This suggests that asking children for their opinions is not something teachers do. Further, my description of the work I was doing as 'messing about' suggests that I was beginning to accept the idea that the only legitimate focus for classroom work was what is laid out in the National Curriculum programmes of study. Other teachers' stories of not having time can also be viewed in this light. Teaching as synonymous with delivery of the National Curriculum was gradually becoming accepted as unarguable, the natural order of things (Moore *et al*, 2002).

The idea that addressing the children's personal and cultural development was increasingly seen as optional, not as fundamental to their education, was captured memorably by Rose. She reflected on a time several years earlier when St Matthew's had a strong reputation for multiculturalism, which had gradually died away, partly because the two teachers at the heart of the initiative left:

> It's like recorder players. If you've got someone who plays recorder, you give the lessons.

Rose's analogy implies that if you don't have someone who plays recorder, you just don't give the lessons. Recorder playing, like multi-culturalism, is a bonus, a luxury item, and not an essential part of the children's entitlement.

I was reminded once again of the source of the pressure to teach in a way which was not necessarily in the best interests of the children by a conversation with the headteacher. Discussing the school's lack of recognition of children's cultural backgrounds it became clear that he was under at least as much pressure as the teachers, and was possibly just as uncomfortable with the compromises he felt forced to make:

> I agree to a point with what you are saying but ultimately things won't change. I'm a pragmatist: I conform to Ofsted criteria to get the inspectors off the back of the staff and the school. If I give them what they want, they will stay away. If I don't I'll bring down a pile of trouble on the staff. Maybe that's the wrong approach but... (shrugs)

By 'giving them what they want' he meant conforming to the Ofsted requirements in terms of the National Curriculum and pressing for continually improving SATs results to maintain a respectable position in local league tables. In his terms, the strategy worked: the school was regarded as a 'light touch' school, requiring little monitoring. But in avoiding official scrutiny, I felt the school paid the price by neglecting the social and cultural needs of the children.

These conversations forced me to rethink my ideas about race as the fundamental problem. I had always been aware of the pressure exerted on us from central government. But I had perhaps not understood how significant that pressure was in controlling not only what was taught and how it was taught, but also in influencing how over time teachers saw their role.

Another issue that arose in conversation with colleagues was one I had not even considered. While not disregarding my emphasis on the effect of being white in a multi-ethnic school, several teachers pointed out the important cross-cutting effect of social class in forging links across racial and ethnic boundaries and also in breaking up the homogeneity implied in the term white.

The significance of social class

Paula explicitly described herself as working class and she saw this as a key feature of her identity as a teacher:

> She said she felt more at home in a school like this, being from a working class background... regardless of race... She said, 'you might have a cultural connection with the children, or it might be an economic one – and I've got the economic one'

Paula saw different class backgrounds as likely to form barriers between teachers and students in much the same way as race:

> She thought middle class teachers working with working class students would have a similar difficulty to white teachers in multicultural schools.

For her there were points of connection between teachers and pupils, based on shared experiences. Talking to her made me see that while I had focused on the differences between me and my pupils, Paula found the similarities more striking:

> In her own education she felt she was regarded as 'factory fodder' alongside most of her classmates. There was a culture in which 'it wasn't done to be overly clever', and so when she went to college... she had a lot of catching up to do. That feeling of 'I can't contribute

because I feel inferior' which she felt then, and still occasionally feels now, was similar, she thought, to the way the children feel, having to negotiate the hurdles of class, and being a minority group.

It was their working class status that was the point of connection for Paula. It was Paula who had spoken of the importance of re-membering that the children at the school were not Pakistani or Bangladeshi: they had been born in Britain, and knew no other way of life. She saw her role as supporting their developing identities as both British and Muslim.

Rose, who also identified herself as working class, saw the children in terms of both their class and ethnicity. In discussing the dif-ficulties in making changes to what she saw as a Eurocentric geo-graphy curriculum, she said with some emotion:

> 'They've got people at the National Curriculum whose job it is... They could organise this – if we could be given links...' [SP: why doesn't this happen?] 'Because England is predominantly white and what do they care? How much do they know or care in the Home Counties? That's very telling isn't it? Home counties? The National Curriculum doesn't take account of children with ESL. They ignore a whole group of people, ignore a whole lot of poten-tial.'

While she saw whiteness as a factor in the content of the National Curriculum, Rose's use of the term Home Counties evokes images of the middle classes. She saw working class children from ethnic minority groups as being doubly disadvantaged in a white, middle class education system. Paula and Rose shared a sense that class prejudice and racism can go hand in hand and, as working class women, they empathised strongly with ethnic minority families.

Amena also raised the subject of social class. She lived locally and regarded herself as working class. In conversation I once asked her if she felt that any school with a strongly religious base would be better for Muslim children than a non-religious school: she thought not. She said she had worked at a school that was religious:

> More religious and more middle class. They don't really want to know. They expect others to conform to what they are... Some schools expect children to leave their culture at the gate.

Like Rose, Amena felt that the difficulties schools pose for children are to do with school cultures being *both* ethnocentric *and* middle class. In describing the religious school she had worked at as 'more religious and more middle class', she seemed to suggest that St Matthew's had less of a problem. Nevertheless, she still felt that barriers existed between the teachers and the pupils. She gave an example from her own teaching to illustrate an approach to school work she thought relevant to the children's lives, an approach she felt was all too rare at the school:

> She told me about a survey of households she had done to supplement what the children had done about who lived in their houses. By asking lunchtime staff as well as teachers, she had come back with a picture that showed the adults in the school living in the same circumstances as the children.

She suggested that middle class teachers tend to exclude the experiences of working class people from their teaching, much as white people exclude the experiences of non-whites. Like Paula and Rose, she saw ethnic minority working class children as experiencing double exclusion. She commented later that my own project suffered from the same limitations, by focusing on teaching staff alone. Amena challenged my middle class assumptions about who had something important to say about these questions. I had justified my lack of contact with non-teaching staff on the basis that the focus of my project was white teachers. Yet those staff would have had interesting perspectives on those white teachers and on the workings of the school as a white middle class institution.

One teacher who referred to the significance of class was herself from a white middle class background. Jane was keenly aware of what she called 'a clash of paradigms' between middle class teachers and working class children. On the subject of conversations I had had with children, she said:

> Teachers are in a position of tremendous power... and I do wonder about this relationship. I mean, you like to think you're liberal, you like to think you've got all the right-on attitudes, and, 'hey she can come to me anytime', but that is not necessarily the way the children see it at all... And so I wonder on whose terms those conversations are, and I think they are very much ours. I think children are

quite fearful of talking about home, or their religion, because they are not sure what kind of reaction they are going to get.

Jane picked up an earlier preoccupation of mine: why don't children talk about home? And she is well aware that it is the messages we send as teachers that prevent them from saying the things on their minds. For her, though, the gap between children and teachers is more to do with power differences, based on both class and the conventional teacher-child relationship, than the cultural and ethnic differences that were my preoccupation.

Islam and gender equality

Another new issue to emerge from my discussions with colleagues was the behaviour and attitudes of the Muslim pupils at the school. Three teachers in particular highlighted the behaviour of Muslim boys as a problem at St Matthew's. Jane was the first to raise the subject. She said she felt strongly about what she called

> ... 'a mismatch between what is sanctioned at home and at school', in terms of the behaviour of Muslim boys and girls. She wondered whether the stereotyped male aggression of the boys could be called Muslim behaviour, and said she suspected it was the result of a different set of expectations at home: 'I radically disapprove of a woman walking four paces behind a man.'

Jane thought that stereotyped male aggression might have something to do with being a Muslim, and appeared to suggest a link between this behaviour and the perceived low status of women and girls in Muslim families. Though Jane was the most uncompromising in highlighting this as a problem, she was not the only teacher to do so. Claire described how, in her first term at the school, a mother had come into school to ask her to discipline her young son because he refused to obey her at home. Her attitude to this was unequivocal:

> How far do I go before I say that as a Western woman I find that unacceptable? To some extent, it's a case of 'when in Rome, do as the Romans do'.

These words tap into two ideas about Muslims that seem common in Western countries. First, Claire called herself a Western woman, and seemed to see her values as in direct opposition to Muslim values: her view was that the West upholds gender equality while Islam denies it. Second, her use of the phrase 'when in Rome, do as the Romans do' suggests that she believed that immigrants should only be allowed to live in Britain if they adopt British norms of behaviour. Responding to Claire's description of the woman who asked for help with her son, Elizabeth described an incident in which a Muslim mother whose son had been hitting and kicking her had asked her for help in controlling him. Her attitude to this was more tentative:

> Where has he got the message that this is OK? It's a minefield, because you don't want to insult anyone, knowing so little about it, and knowing families aren't all the same: some are more fundamentalist than others.' She spoke of the increased status of women in the west, and the feeling that this isn't recognised by some of the fathers, though this was not simply Muslim men, but an issue for all men. She had heard British-born educated Mums saying things like, 'our men are dreadful'.

In this incident Elizabeth described herself as unsure how to act because she does not know how strongly fundamentalist the family in question was. The implication appears to be that if they were, they would think that boys' violence toward their mothers was acceptable, so if she intervened she would be challenging their religious values. On the other hand she was aware that Muslims differ over the role of women and that it would be wrong to assume that all Muslims were misogynistic. She added that misogyny is not just a problem for Islam, and spoke of other groups of women struggling with negative male attitudes.

As a teacher of mainly seven and eight year olds, I was not strongly aware then of any overt male arrogance or aggression from the boys at the school. However, some time later I covered a lesson with a class of ten and eleven year olds for an absent colleague. Except for one white and one African-Caribbean boy in the class, all were South Asian Muslims:

> There was a very distinct 'lad culture' going on in the room. I had felt it very strongly when working in a parallel class last term, and this class had the same edgy atmosphere. Several times I felt some of the boys were trying to patronise me, to undermine my authority.

I found this particularly disturbing since I had taught many of the boys as seven year olds and had anticipated friendliness and respect that were not forthcoming. I recorded on that morning, and at other times in this class, several examples of disrespectful attitudes to girls in the class too. The following example was typical, though others were more offensive:

> Salma was sitting backwards on her chair, 'cowboy style'. Rizwan looked at her and said, to no one in particular, 'Look at her – put your legs together, you're sitting like a man.'

It seemed to me that Rizwan referred to Salma's lack of femininity to shame her into behaving in what he considered to be a more appropriate way. This could be seen as a sexist remark that could have been made by any child. Indeed, some years earlier, in a mainly white school, a white girl had approached me to complain that her female classmate was sitting in exactly this way, as if it were obvious that she was doing something wrong. That the comment was a direct instruction: 'put your legs together', rather than an observation, may suggest that Rizwan felt he had a right to speak to Salma in this way. Could this have been due to his perceived higher status as a Muslim or South Asian boy? Nevertheless, Salma did not adjust her pose.

My comment on this incident at the time was:

> This is how we learn what is and is not acceptable to our gender, then. I suppose it was equally possible that a girl would jeer at a boy for crying?

This comment suggests that at the time I saw it as an example of gender stereotyping rather than anything to do with Islam.

Raj, a British Indian newly qualified teacher who taught in the parallel class to the one mentioned above, also had difficulties with some of the boys, but saw this as due to her own ethnicity:

> She sometimes got the feeling the boys thought, 'she's only like my auntie or my sister. I don't have to listen to her.'

Raj was obviously referring to the Muslim boys, though she is a Hindu. Was she right in assuming that her own ethnic background made the boys less respectful to her than to white teachers? Was the disrespect she experienced simply a challenge to her authority, common to newly qualified teachers, or was it the less tangible sense of disrespect that I had experienced in the parallel class that morning? In this case, it is not ethnicity which is influencing the boys' attitudes but gender.

Amena had also encountered what she regarded as a disrespectful attitude to women from some of the boys, but she made it clear that she felt it was not all the boys, and not all Muslims:

> It's the Bengali boys. They have a problem with dealing with women.

Several teachers mentioned some boys' disrespectful behaviour toward women and girls as a problem at the school. Jane, Claire and, to some extent, Elizabeth saw it as a problem related to Islam. Raj and Amena tended to feel it was more to do with the boys' ethnic backgrounds. My own view of the incident with Salma and Rizwan was that the main issue was gender rather than religion or culture, though I did wonder about the effect of culture on Rizwan's authoritative instruction to Salma. Other teachers tended to share my view that it was the boys' developing ideas about masculinity that mainly caused the problem.

While some teachers were concerned about the aggressive behaviour of the boys, their attitude to the girls was often centred on their perceived lack of ambition. When I asked what the children spoke of doing with their lives, most teachers spontaneously divided the children by gender when responding:

> Raj: The pressure is on boys especially. There is much less interest in the girls being ambitious, unfortunately.

> Rose: To be a mum, which disturbs me. Other than that there were a variety of ambitions.

> Jane: Most girls who mention it see a domestic future, though occasionally medicine is mentioned.

> Paula: Most want to be wives and mothers. There is cultural pressure – though there are exceptions.

> Elizabeth: There are an enormous amount of girls who are going to be mums. It's very stereotyped. I don't know if it would be the same in other schools, perhaps so.

It is difficult to interpret these comments because although the teachers do differentiate between boys and girls, most make no reference to ethnicity in discussing the girls' attitudes. Yet between 80 and 90 per cent of the children at the school were from Muslim backgrounds. The teachers' comments may be informed by a stereotype of South Asian girls as likely to marry early and have no interest in a career. But they all also point to some small variation in this pattern, or, as in the final comment, to the fact that the reasons for the lack of ambition may be unrelated to culture or religion. Indeed several girls demonstrated to me that they were thinking ahead and planning to do well, though there were others who had not yet considered anything other than motherhood in their future. As with the boys, it is tempting to relate certain behaviours to the most obvious, most visible source: Islam. But it may be that in the case of both the boys' misogyny and the girls' perceived lack of ambition, gender, class, family histories and education levels, as well as our own preconceptions and priorities as teachers, may be more significant factors than religion. Some of the teachers had already pointed out the way in which social class influenced teacher-pupil relationships. And many of the parents who sent their children to St Matthews had themselves grown up in remote rural areas of Pakistan and Bangladesh and had received little formal education. It may have been this, and not the fact that they were Muslims, which was more influential in shaping their views of appropriate behaviour in men and women.

Stereotyping

Many of the teachers at St Matthew's were aware of the stereotypes that exist about different ethnic groups and often resisted them. The few stereotypical references made were usually aimed at the Muslim children – but then they formed the vast majority of the school population.

Research studies have demonstrated that teachers – often unconsciously – adopt stereotypes of children based on their behaviour or academic performance. Some indicate that teachers have an unconscious model of the ideal pupil in their heads against which they judge the children in their class (e.g. Gillborn, 1990, Youdell, 2003). Race, gender and social class all play an important part in the judgements teachers make about children, and this initial judgement influences their developing relationship. While many writers and researchers agree that stereotyping is a significant problem, few would claim that all teachers stereotype pupils, or that those who do are overtly racist, sexist or elitist. What the research does suggest is that stereotyping is a subtle and complex process of which teachers are largely unaware.

One way of understanding ethnic stereotypes is to think of what has been called an 'archive of knowledge' (Young, 2000), a store of myths and prejudices that people possess about ethnic groups other than their own. One common feature of the myths that surround black and Asian people in the West is that they tend to give both sex and race exaggerated prominence: there is no way of being that is not related to one or both for members of visible minority groups. Stereotypes of black men include images of aggression and sexual promiscuity, while Asian women are seen as alluringly submissive, for example. Walter Mosley, an African-American crime novelist, tells the story of the time he tried to get his first novel featuring a black detective published, only to be told that there was already a black detective in the world of crime fiction and that he should come up with a more original idea. While the many white detectives are defined by their idiosyncrasies – Sherlock Holmes' superiority complex, for example, or Morse's highbrow tastes – to be black is sufficient to define a character. Stereotypes caricature and simplify: they allow others to view people from minority groups as typical examples of their group, not as complex individuals.

Recent research studies have found that the view of South Asian girls as passive and lacking in ambition is extremely common among teachers. Basit (1997) suggests that this misunderstanding occurred among the white teachers in her study because they consistently misconstrued the behaviour of the Muslim girls in their classes. What the girls saw as respectfulness was perceived as submissiveness, and what their parents saw as protectiveness was interpreted as oppression. She suggests that this lack of understanding was a result of the teachers judging the girls' behaviour according to their – usually white – norms. This suggestion is supported by how teachers see the hijab as a symbol of backwardness and oppression (Zine, 2000) and regard time spent away from school for Eid celebrations and visits to Pakistan as inappropriate (Bigger, 2000). Such views are an expression of a particular, in this case Western, cultural standpoint, and are not neutral.

Basit (1997) found that the educational and career aspirations among the Muslim girls in her study were high: almost all wanted to go on to further and higher education, and then to a profession, in direct contrast to their teachers' perceptions of them as future mothers and housewives only. Basit points to a strong sense of class prejudice in these assumptions, of which the Asian teachers at the school were equally guilty.

While stereotypes about Muslim girls are only now beginning to change, ideas about Muslim boys have undergone a significant transformation over the past decade. Most studies in the 1990s found that teachers regarded Asian boys of all religions as well be-haved and hard working (e.g. Connolly, 1998). However, parental expectations for their sons were still seen as unrealistic, despite their success at school, a finding which suggests similar class-based expectations to those experienced by the girls. More recent studies, however, have highlighted the emergence of a new stereotype: that of Asian boys as the most challenging ethnic sub-group. Mac an Ghaill (1994) may have been the first to note this change, suggesting that Muslim boys were beginning to replace African-Caribbean boys in teachers' perceptions as the most difficult group in school, and were certainly perceived to be the most sexist ethnic group. Since then Bhatti (1999) has reported Asian boys being unjustly punished in similar ways to their African-Caribbean classmates, and that teachers believed Asian boys in general lacked respect for women. Shain (2003) suggests that these new ideas reflect changes in wider ethnic stereotypes about Muslims as backward and fanatical, which began in the late 1980s and have gained in currency as a result of the events of September 11 2001.

At St Matthew's, some of the boys did sometimes seem dismissive and disrespectful to female classmates and even, on occasion, female teachers. But relating the problem to perceived unequal gender roles in Islam is hardly a productive way of tackling it. Indeed, part of the problem could be said to be how little many non-Muslim teachers understand about Islam and the ethnic, cultural and geographical backgrounds of their pupils. For a start, the widespread Western view of Islam as a monolithic religion in which all Muslims share an identical set of beliefs is wholly inaccurate (Fawsi El-Solh and Mabro, 1994). Like all major global religions, Islam is practiced in different ways in different countries, and is affected by cultural, ethnic and political influences (Yamani, 1996). The debate about the position of women in Islam is complex, but the Qu'ran certainly speaks of the equality of men and women before God, and in many Islamic cultures women's education is considered important. Teachers should also be aware that there is no single rule on the role of women in the many Islamic societies of the world, nor in the many different Islamic communities in Western countries (Ask and Tjomsland, 1998). Ideas about what is appropriate behaviour for women – and indeed for men – are just as bound up in different social and cultural traditions as in religious ones. The tradition of arranged marriage, for example, does not come from the Qu'ran.

Perhaps the most high profile example of Western misunderstandings of women in Islam is centred around the wearing of the hijab, or veil. The question of whether Islam requires women to cover their bodies wholly or extensively is a matter of interpretation of the Qu'ran and other key religious texts, and interpretations vary widely (Ask and Tjomsland, *ibid*). In the West, the hijab has come to symbolise Muslim women's oppression, and there are Muslim women who share this view. Yet many women are taking up the hijab as a public sign of a personal commitment to Islam, sometimes regardless of their own family's practice (Ask and Tjomsland, 1998). It can therefore become an emblem of independence. Once again, what teachers need to do is put aside their own cultural preconceptions and try to see the issue from the Muslim women and girls' point of view.

None of this implies that gender inequality is not a problem in Muslim societies – it is. But many Muslim women are clear that their goals may not be the same as those of women in the West, and that in achieving them they are prepared neither to reject their religion nor to embrace Western values as superior to their own

(Yamani, 1996). While conservative interpretations of aspects of Islam are indeed oppressive to women, the abuse or marginalisation of women comes in many forms and is very much in evidence in Christianity and secular Western society too, though it may not always be recognised as such (Fawsi El-Solh and Mabro, 1994). In coming to understand these matters, non-Muslim teachers may be better able to confront misogyny in all its guises and in all pupils.

The problem with stereotyping is that it fixes people into positions that are not really fixed. Neither culture nor religion ever stay the same: both are constantly changing. There are two problems with the view of some of the teachers at St Matthews that Islam was the reason for the children's behaviour. The first is that it suggests that Islam is a completely unified religion, in which all Muslims believe the same thing. This is clearly not the case, as Elizabeth notes. The second is that because they saw Islam as ultimately responsible for the boys' aggression or the girls' lack of effort, the teachers were unwilling to tackle either for fear of being accused of at best cultural insensitivity or at worst racism. Consequently there was little open discussion of the problem among the staff, though such a dialogue would have been very illuminating, since teachers from different backgrounds had such different ideas. Some believed the key problem was religious, others that it was cultural, and others that class or levels of education was the most significant issue.

Abbas' research (2002) suggests that raising the issue of boys' anti-social behaviour and girls' underachievement without assuming that it has something to do with religion may be more productive. He found two secondary schools in which teachers had highlighted the pattern of sexism among Muslim boys and lack of ambition among girls that existed at St Matthew's. But in these schools the teachers viewed both of these behaviours as due to cultural rather than religious influences. The teachers refused to see religious or cultural identities as uniform or unchanging and non-negotiable, and had begun to work with families to improve both the boys' behaviour and the girls' achievements. The study suggests that teachers who believe that inappropriate behaviour stems from traditional cultural rather than religious beliefs are more willing to work with parents and children to change those beliefs, because they do not believe they are challenging religious precepts.

Some teachers at St Matthew's did reject the idea that the children's gendered behaviour was related to their religion. Paula stated unequivocally that gender stereotypes exist in all ethnic groups:

> 'Boys believe they're very much in charge of the world. Some bolshie girls want to challenge that' ... She saw boys as more assertive and girls more passive, but didn't think it had anything to do with ethnicity: it was the same across all cultural groups. 'It's hard to get them out of that thinking.'

Just as she saw it as part of her role to push children to achieve at school, Paula's statement that 'it's hard to get them out of that thinking' indicates her sense of obligation to challenge gender stereotypes in the classroom, whatever their origin. Rose shared this attitude:

> She told me about an incident when they had been writing a play about Cinderella as a class. She deliberately inserted the line, 'have a rest Cinderella, the boys can clean the house' to see what the reaction of the boys in the class would be. They had just laughed – no one said 'boys don't do that'. It was not the response she had anticipated.

Rose knew that the boys and girls in her class already saw themselves as having different roles to play, and, like Paula, she saw it as part of her role to challenge this view. She did so in a relatively playful way, by inserting the provocative line 'the boys can clean the house'. She apparently intended that line to stimulate a debate about gender roles in the home, which, to her surprise, did not come about. She did not mention an ethnic or cultural basis for this stereotypical view of their roles.

Owning up to racism

One of the aspects of my behaviour I found hardest to come to terms with was my lack of understanding of what racism is and how it works. Like many white people who tend not to have to deal with racism on a regular basis, I began by seeing racism as a fairly rare individual character defect. It took some time before I began to understand how racism can be built into society and institutions, and how it works to disadvantage minority groups in ways the majority group may be oblivious of. Talking with the colleagues who had become most closely involved with my project, it was clear that there was a division between those who saw racism as to do with individual prejudice, and those who saw it as a much more complex and pervasive feature of life. The first mention in the discussion of racism was very subtle. Rose was discussing her difficulty with the changing terminology of race. All the participants in the conversation were white:

> Rose: At one time to call somebody 'black' was highly offensive, you had to say 'coloured,' and then it was 'coloured' that was highly offensive. And you felt, 'I don't want to be seen as causing offence'. It gets in the way of people, it gets in the way of who the person is.
>
> Laura: They see the colour before anything else don't they?
>
> Rose: Yes...and that's what we think about, don't we?

Rose seemed to be saying that she could not keep up with the changing terminology of race so felt confused rather than empowered by it. But what seems more significant is the attitude to racism that Rose and Laura reveal in this brief exchange. The comment made by Laura, that '*they* see colour before anything else', suggests that she assumes that no one in the room could be seen as capable of racism. Rose responds by agreeing to the proposition that there is a tendency to judge people by the colour of their skin, but says 'that's what *we* think about'. Her use of 'we' instead of 'they' suggests that she does not agree that the people in the room are necessarily free of racist attitudes. She differs from Laura in acknowledging the existence of unconscious racism.

Other colleagues also recognised the influence of racism on their thinking. Later in the same discussion Paula and Kaye each told a story in which they were implicated in subtly racist acts. Again, everyone taking part in the conversation was white:

> Paula: We went to America, and we went over the Mexican border, and there was a gang (look I'm doing it now)... I mean three or four Mexican men, and they were like the Mexican men that you see in the films – checked shirts, jeans, the little hairnet things on their heads. And straight away I went like that with my bag [mimes placing hand protectively over it]. And I thought, 'what have I done that for?' You can't legislate for that, can you...? I didn't consciously do it, but then I thought, 'why on earth have I done that?'

[nods from a few others in the group]

Kaye: I remember, when I was pregnant, Steve and I were walking home... and there was this group of black guys walking towards us, and Steve stood in front of me, and he said afterwards he was protecting me, because I was pregnant ...and these guys sort of approached and said, 'have you got the time?' And he was horrified, when we got home he said, 'why did I do that?' And he said he was protecting me because I was more vulnerable than normal...

Laura: Was that because they were black, or because it was a group?

Kaye: I don't know, but he was horrified with himself, that he had acted in that way.

Rose: I've done that with white men as well.

Maggie: My son has had that. I've seen him standing on the corner with his friends. We know he's not doing anything, but I've seen old ladies look at them, and cross the road. You see a group, even just two or three, and you think... [makes a face indicating concern or fear].

The women who told these stories accepted that underlying these defensive actions had been racist thinking, and both Paula and Kaye's husband Steve openly acknowledged and rejected this aspect of their make-up. Paula is particularly reflective about her attitude, noting her own pejorative use of the word gang as she tells the story. Her rhetorical question, 'you can't legislate for that, can you?' suggests that she acknowledges the power of racist attitudes to infiltrate her thinking, even though she considered herself to be non-racist or even antiracist. Laura's question about whether Steve had acted as he did because the men were black or because they were in a group is a valid one, and Maggie's account of her son and his white friends being perceived as threatening is also relevant. Yet the fact that the group did not accept that the incidents *might* have been racist suggests that these comments were made in an attempt to disprove the racist aspects of the stories. In other words, in telling their stories about groups of young white men as a counterweight to Paula and Kaye's stories, Maggie and Rose were trying to suggest that racism was not at the root of their fear, even though the women themselves were willing to admit that it was.

What seems to me to be happening here is that two different conceptions of racism are at work. Paula and Kaye saw their stories of racist reactions as symptomatic of living in a racially structured society. Though they took responsibility for their actions and disapproved of them, they saw them as an example of how white people unconsciously get caught up in racism. In contrast, others in the group who understood racism as an individual character flaw admitting to racist feelings in this way naturally felt that was far more risky. According to their understanding of racism, Paula and Kaye would be admitting to being unpleasant, anti-social people. At the heart of the difference is the view of ourselves as either free agents who choose our attitudes and behaviour, or as individuals caught up in a wider social network which to some extent shapes and defines us. This more sociological, or political, view of their role as teachers seemed to me to be a key point of contrast between the teachers who were more confident about race and difference in the classroom and those, like me, who still struggled with inhibition and fear.

5

Teaching as a Political Activity

You might have a cultural connection with the children, or it might be an economic one – and I've got the economic one.

peaking to the teachers enabled me to see aspects of the situation I couldn't see alone. But some of my colleagues appeared much more confident than others about dealing with race and difference, and much clearer in their minds about their role as teachers in this diverse community. I was able to learn a great deal from these women about how to teach with greater confidence and sensitivity.

New perspectives on what good teaching is and should be had first emerged when conversation turned to social class. Rose and Paula had described themselves as working class, and felt strongly that their backgrounds enabled them better to understand the obstacles in the way of the working class South Asian children they now taught. Amena was conscious of sharing an experience of exclusion on the grounds of both class *and* race. All three women had strong views on how gender affects educational opportunity. Because they had experienced difficulties as a result of their class, gender or race and, in Amena's case, all three, they were clear that society was structured according to these social identities. It was natural to use their own experiences of marginalisation to understand the barriers likely to be placed in the way of their pupils.

But there were other routes to greater awareness. Kaye came from a middle class background, but her political inclinations brought her to London when antiracist education was high on the agenda, and she had always felt comfortable in multi-ethnic settings. Each of these women, and others at the school, had ideas on being a better teacher and therefore a better teacher in a diverse classroom. Returning to Frankenberg's framework of the three attitudes to race, one feature of their teaching which seemed to unite these different women was their colour and power cognisant approach to their work in the classroom.

Being racialised

Most white people do not give a great deal of thought to race. Just as gender tends to be seen as mainly to do with women, race is often seen as mainly concerning ethnic minority groups. When I began this project I saw myself as a neutral outsider, who would help children from ethnic minorities. My initial focus was on *their* problems with race and culture. I did not see those problems as having anything to do with me. I now believe that this was because I did not see myself as having a race in the same way they did. I was just normal: they were different, and that was where the problems lay. But like it or not, we have all been assigned to a race: we are all racialised. Our race can determine how people treat us, though the extent of this varies from context to context. In Western countries, where being white means you are part of the majority, this is very easy to forget.

I spoke to nine teachers at the school about their attitudes to race. Both Amena and Raj, the only ones from ethnic minority groups, mentioned race as a feature of their childhoods. Raj's parents came from India and she was born and raised in the North of England.

> Throughout her school life, until sixth form college, Raj and her sister were 'practically the only coloured faces in the school'. She enjoyed school, and had very little trouble with racism, though this was not the case for her sister.

Raj's memory of being a rarity at school, and her almost casual reference to the 'very little' racism she encountered, especially compared with her sister, illustrates how being marked as racially different affected her experience of school.

For Amena there was a direct link between her family's experiences and her feelings about what children should learn in school:

> Her father was a policeman, and an overseer of a plantation before coming to Britain, but then had to drive a bus. 'We don't cover those things... we need to deal with things that really hit home, that they'll have to do with.'

Amena spoke from personal experience of the common pattern of skilled people coming from Commonwealth countries to find work in Britain, only to find that they were not accepted in positions of the kind they held in their home countries. They had to accept the jobs white people did not want, not because of lack of education but because of the way high status jobs were kept for white people. This knowledge unsurprisingly led Amena to view disadvantage in terms of both class and race, since her family had been forced to accept a lower class position when they came to Britain because of their race. As a black African Muslim, Amena had to cope with being seen as different both in the mainstream white society and in the local Muslim community. She knew of the many forms that racism may take, and had more than once spoken of racism among Muslims in general, and of the segregation by Muslims into their various ethnic groups in the local mosques.

Only two of the seven white teachers mentioned race as having a significant impact on their early lives. This is to be expected: we only become aware of ourselves when we meet people who are different from us. The idea of being a girl has little meaning until it is compared to being a boy. Children from ethnic minority groups growing up in a mainly white society are likely to be much more conscious of difference than their white counterparts, especially those who grew up in relatively homogenous areas. Yet the fact that two white teachers did see race as significant in their early lives offers a way of discovering how and why some white teachers develop greater awareness than others of their own racial identity.

Kaye was one of these two teachers. She described a childhood in the 1960s spent in 'a traditional Anglo Saxon village'. This description signals that Kaye was – somewhat humorously – conscious of the significance of her racial background. She said that though most of the people around her had been white at primary school she had gravitated toward the two non-white children in her class.

It didn't cross her mind that there was any difference between the three of them until she was thirteen or fourteen. It wasn't until she moved to London that she mixed with people from different cultures in large numbers...she said she had always been a bit 'right on'... had always had those kinds of attitudes and opinions.

Rose, who was in her fifties, talked about growing up in a fairly diverse inner-city area in the 1950s. She remembered the first time she had become aware of racism:

Her best friend at school had an Asian mother and an Irish father, though she didn't remember noticing her colour until they were thirteen. The friend had invited a boy she liked to her birthday party, but the boy had not come. Rose said she remembered wondering for the first time whether this might be because of her colour.

So only the two white teachers who spoke of noticing race in childhood had developed close friendships with children from minority groups. Possibly it helped them see the world through the eyes of their friends and notice the subtle racism they faced, as in Rose's example of the boy who did not come to her friend's party.

These early experiences obviously influenced Rose and Kaye's understanding of race, although the greater awareness can come later. Paula's story of her own unconscious racism toward a group of Mexican men while on holiday in the US indicates that one can become aware of how race structures our lives at any time. But it happens most forcibly from personal experience.

Acknowledging racism

Some teachers saw racism as a bigger problem than others did. I asked almost all the teachers about racism at St Matthew's. Most responded by talking about racist incidents between children, and one referred to racist parents at the school. But Rose and Paula responded differently. In answer to my question about whether she saw racism as a problem at St Matthew's, Rose said:

It must be – for the children. It encroaches on their lives outside, and it must encroach inside, though I don't see it... I'm trying to think of incidents which were specifically racist. There must be racist taunts, but if there are they must be kept quite hidden. I know the children have had things shoved through letter boxes, see things on walls.

dren. She brought home to me the weakness in my own early approach, which despite my good intentions, still tended to keep people at arm's length:

> You have to be with the people. You can't just read it in books. Travel and talking to other people gives you greater understanding ... unless you talk to people you won't really understand.

Some teachers seemed to know this instinctively. Paula was the only teacher working with the older pupils who would always go out to the playground with her class at the end of the day, to chat to parents and children, and to the teachers of the younger children who brought their classes out as a matter of course. Again physical distance stands as a metaphor for social distance. Teachers who come into the playground are making themselves available for a quiet chat or a quick joke. The playground is neutral; there is far less of a distinction between teacher and parent, whereas teachers who stay in the classroom remain within the institution: inaccessible, hidden, and parents must venture into unfamiliar territory to find them.

Paula's habit of coming out to meet the parents each day was based on her respect for them and their role in the children's education:

> The parents have high expectations, and respect for education. They know their children will be disadvantaged, and that education is a way to right those wrongs.

As bell hooks (1992, p170) notes, 'stereotypes abound when there is distance'. In the absence of personal relationships and first hand knowledge on which to base our judgements, we fall back on stereotypes. It is, as Paula knew, a common assumption among teachers that parents who did not themselves have extensive education are not interested in their children doing well academically. But personal experience had taught her that this is far from true. Once a network of relationships is established, stereotypes fall away as meaningless and trite in the face of the complexity of individual lives. There was something about the way that some teachers saw their role as teachers that made them more inclined to build strong relationships with their pupils and the pupils' families.

In our conversations, some teachers resisted all attempts, including by me, to make generalisations about the children. Paula was adamant that one could not treat Muslim children as if they all believed the same thing and followed the same practices. She felt she knew her class of ten and eleven year olds very well:

> 'Like all religions there are different degrees of feeling – some don't go to mosque at all – it's not good to lump them all into one group, everyone is an individual'... She found that in her class there were always three or four children well versed in Islam, and another half a dozen who knew quite a lot. 'The rest just nod a lot'.

Rose remembered the impact the Rushdie affair had had on the children. The disrespectful depiction of Islam in Salman Rushdie's novel, *The Satanic Verses*, caused huge offence among many Muslims during the late 1980s, and this was compounded by the fact that he could not be prosecuted under British law. The Ayatollah in Iran issued a *fatwah* or death threat to the author, and he had to go into hiding. It was a time of intense debate and serious hostility between Muslim and non-Muslim communities, both nationally and locally. Rose compared this period with the time before and since, when working at the school seemed 'perfectly natural and comfortable'. But during the Rushdie affair a few families had held views she found unacceptable:

> No parents had said anything to her, but three different children had said, 'we cannot celebrate Eid until he is dead'. Rose had been horrified by this, and was very conscious of a divide. Still, she felt, 'there are extremists of every nationality and faith, and you could be in a white area and hear equally horrendous things'.

Rose sees the children who said they wanted Rushdie to die as voicing an extremist, rather than common view among Muslims. She also acknowledges that such extremism is to be found in all social groups. She was not the only teacher who was horrified by a few of the children's comments, though she acknowledged that they were far from typical. Because of the stereotypical notion that Muslims are all fundamentalists, there is the danger that people who hear a child speak in this way will assume this view is a basic and unchallengeable feature of the religion, so feel both deeply hostile to Islam and unable to act for fear of being seen as racist. Linking such attitudes to race or religion makes it difficult to confront it. The teachers who were more successful in challenging unacceptable behaviour were those who felt it had nothing to do with religion or race, and dealt with aggression, racism or sexism as an infringement of school rules.

Influencing children's life choices

Closely linked to the notion some teachers shared that they were no different than their pupils was the idea that they had a right to influence the life choices they made. As well as keeping my personal life out of the classroom, I rarely had conversations with children about what they wanted to do with theirs. Though I believed strongly in education as a way of giving children opportunities they might not otherwise have had, I did not intervene to urge them to work harder or to point to what they might achieve. Again it is difficult now to see why. Did I believe that at eight and nine they were too young for careers advice? Was it simply that I was too busy with the curriculum? Or did I subconsciously think that I might stir up controversy by urging them to do things they might not be permitted, or able, to do? Did I have stereotypical assumptions, based on race or class or both, about what was possible for these children?

Paula certainly did not share these inhibitions. She was, as usual, the most articulate and uncompromising in her stance:

> I say, 'change things – don't go and work in Asda.' She remembers her own education, and her lack of ambition, and urges the children to get out of that situation. I say to them things like, 'I could give up this job and go and work in Australia if I wanted to, because I've got an education – so could you'. 'It drives me mental when they say 'I want to work in Asda'. They know it's not a good job – they don't think they're clever enough to be doctors. I say, 'is that what your mum wants?' and they say, 'no, she wants me to be a doctor', and I say, 'yes, well!'

As well as being confident of her right to speak to the children in this way, Paula believed in working alongside parents to enable the children to succeed against what she saw as the double disadvantage of race and class :

> 'The teachers here see that too. Maybe that's why they put out more.' In white schools there can be the feeling 'well, what can we

do with these kids?' And there used to be a bit of that here, but things have changed.

Paula was referring to the culture of low expectations among teachers in some schools which serve less privileged communities, and admitted that it had been a problem at St Matthew's in the past. But she felt the staff as a whole were now more committed to raising the pupils' achievement.

Rose shared Paula's belief that it is part of the teacher's role to push children to succeed: 'I keep saying, 'remember – you can do anything'.' Kaye said she always made a point of asking parents at parents' meetings what they wanted for their children:

> 'They would say, 'college, and a profession'. She laughed: 'I say, 'well get them to school every day then'!

Elizabeth, who worked with the youngest children, also felt she had a role in opening up future prospects and allowing all the children, especially the girls, to see what opportunities existed. When I asked what the children said to her about their ambitions, she remembered:

> Two have said teachers. Not much else for girls. After I did a speech about women working, I got dentists, etc. Boys say either WWF or football, the occasional taxi driver, or shopkeeper. There's not usually much in the way of high ambition. I don't know how much one might expect from five, six, seven year olds. Some girls name a job and add, 'and a mum', which is fine.'

Elizabeth said she had only recently realised that she should talk more about future choices, and started doing it 'bringing in a bit of feminism. You have to'.

Elizabeth's discussion with her class reveals a little about how children begin to think about their futures. They can only select from the options they see before them. Thus the choices are teaching, which they are familiar with, the fantasy roles they see performed on TV, or the jobs their family members do. So teachers can be immensely influential in broadening the range of options children have access to. Elizabeth was aware of this and had begun to extend her young class' awareness of the future opportunities that might be available.

My reaction to these conversations told me as much about myself as the conversations tell me about these women. At first I saw their attitude as rather intrusive. Was it not presumptuous of them to think they had the right to tell children not to work in a supermarket, or to be so blunt about telling parents to get their children to school? I saw that this was another reason I had not taken a more interventionist approach. I did not see the role of the teacher extending that far.

But Kaye, Rose, Amena and Paula were among the teachers who saw it as an integral part of their role as teachers to challenge the children to succeed, to make them aware of the obstacles they might meet, and to encourage and urge them to overcome them. Some of the teachers drew on direct experience, having themselves got an education in circumstances where to do so was unusual. Their approach was fundamentally political. They saw themselves as activists: they saw education as a vehicle for social change. And these same teachers were among those who took the most critical view of the changes in education policy over the years. They knew that education is a profoundly political activity, not an unproblematic process of passing on a neutral or agreed body of knowledge (King, 2001). Other teachers, who cared just as deeply for the children, did not see their work in this way and were consequently less inclined to resist the pressure to conform to the prevailing ethos.

6

Conclusion

The significance of whiteness

The five years in which I kept a diary at St Matthew's have been the richest and most personally rewarding of my career. I learned a great deal about myself and my strengths and weaknesses as a teacher. My changing perception of the nature of the problems I faced in the classroom documented in the diary shows how my understanding of the teaching process deepened and became more personal over time. I began with the idea that I was part of the solution to a problem outside myself: that the problem was the children's difficulty in coming to terms with their dual identities. And I was determined to help them.

Gradually I began to see that there were at least two significant obstacles to this happy solution. First, the curriculum was not designed to enable children from minority groups to understand their place in the world. Second, the school was required to treat the children as if they were white monolingual English speakers. Understanding these problems helped me take a more realistic view of what could be achieved, but I still saw myself as the solution to the problem and not part of the problem itself. I did acknowledge, however, that my teaching needed to change so as to overcome the narrowness of the curriculum. And as I tracked the changes I made in my diary, it occurred to me that my own behaviour was just as significant as the children's in determining what and how they learned.

At first I felt that the problem was that I was a white teacher amid children from a variety of non-white backgrounds. I saw things only from a white perspective; I used examples only from white cultural sources; I felt uncomfortable about addressing race and racism *because* I was white. And this meant that the children could not relate to me. Nor could they relate to the material I was presenting them with. And I felt sure that other teachers were experiencing the same problems. It was at this, my most evangelical period, that I became involved in Inclusion Week, which I saw as a way of persuading my colleagues to acknowledge what I had just begun to see: the limitations we placed on children because of our lack of knowledge, because of our whiteness.

Some of the reactions to Inclusion Week forced me to think again. The focus on race alone during the week was a problem for some of my colleagues. Raj's choice of Helen Keller as a role model reminded me that there are dangers in highlighting only one form of exclusion. Claire's more direct objections to the exclusion of white people from the week's activities raised a question in my mind about how white people can be made to feel that there is something for them too in inclusion. My uneasiness was compounded by some of the white children's responses to being confronted with white racism.

These reactions from colleagues and pupils forced me to see that things were more complex than I had thought, and I began to think again about my focus on whiteness. Raj's silent protest against the exclusive focus on race reminded me of Edward Said's comment: 'the worst gift of imperialism was allowing people to believe that they were only, main, exclusively, white, or black, or Oriental' (Said, 1993, p407-8). We cannot – any of us – be defined by our skin colour, nor by our religion, culture or ethnicity. These aspects of our identity are cut across by gender, age, social class, where we grew up, our education and our individual biographies, among other factors. And each of these different aspects of ourselves may be more or less important in different contexts. Speaking to lifelong

Londoners makes me aware of my provincial background. Some friends make me more conscious of my gender than others do. When I talk to ethnically diverse groups about race I am always acutely conscious of my whiteness; at other times I forget it. We all experience this re-ordering of our identities in our day-to-day lives, and yet we sometimes reject this understanding of ourselves as having different identities at different times. Perhaps it is rather frightening to live without these certainties: who, beyond my family can I feel close to if those whom I once thought shared my race are no longer obviously like me? My answer is that they never were much more like me than those others whom I used to assume were obviously *not* like me (Baumann, 1999)).

If race is only one aspect of our identities and we are influenced in innumerable ways by other aspects of identity, does a focus on whiteness still make sense? I think it does, because it is only as a result of examining white attitudes to race alongside other racial groups that we can understand how race impacts on our thinking.

One of the most significant effects of whiteness as a racial identity is, paradoxically, the way it makes white people feel they have no racial identity whatsoever (Dyer, 1997). Many white people see themselves as culturally and ethnically neutral, as uninvolved in issues of race or ethnicity. Understanding themselves as set apart from the racialisation of society, the only roles available to them are those of racists, passive observers or altruists: as whites they have no innate right to speak on matters of race (Bonnett, 2000). My own initial idea of this project as being solely for the benefit of the children and as having no resonance for my own life is an example of this approach. One significant contribution work on whiteness can make to race relations is to enable white people to see themselves as having a racial identity that, like all racial identities, impacts on the way they see the world and their place within it.

The stories of inhibition and guilt related here by white teachers indicate what many of us have lost as a consequence of not acknowledging an involvement in issues of race. It has been suggested that the appropriate response to this situation is to cultivate a degree of rage against the racialisation process which has allowed white people to feel they have no positive role on issues of race and therefore must remain silent (Spivak and Harasym, 1990). I came ultimately to understand that in feeling unable to speak, I was feeling the consequences of the racialised nature of society at a personal level for the first time. And having finally felt the force of that structure, I was able to begin the painstaking day to day work of identifying and then challenging it – as a participant, not a neutral observer.

The lack of attention to whiteness as a racial category impacts negatively on white people in another way also. All whites are often assumed to share certain attitudes and behaviours. This was brought home to me when I began interviewing my white colleagues. It seems that when I initially approached them, I assummed they would think as I did, because they like me were white. Some forced me to re-think this assumption by emphasising the importance of social class as a key element of both their own sense of identity and their ability to identify with the children at St Matthew's, despite the differences in racial or ethnic background. Others emphasised aspects of their work which I had not considered significant. Even in this small, close-knit and ethnically similar group of people, the differences between us were vast.

While whiteness is an appropriate focus for understanding teachers in the classroom, one should not be simplistic. Research in the US and Britain on the impact of race awareness courses on white participants suggests that a focus on whiteness as an innately privileged racial identity can provoke a negative response (Gaine, 2001; King, 2001; Levine-Rasky, 2000). It seems that such courses fail because they make it difficult for white people to understand how they can ever escape an identity which is associated with racism and oppression. The idea of disowning whiteness, which is a major theme of such work (e.g. Pearce, 2003), often leads to a feeling of personal guilt about the history of white oppression, or to resentment at being made to feel guilty about the colour of one's skin. Both responses are counter-productive. They offer participants no alternative approach to understanding their situation, an approach which would help them change their perceptions without feeling personally to blame.

An approach that targets a particular set of attitudes and assumptions rather than an entire social group offers better potential for change. The framework of attitudes to race adopted by Frankenberg (1993) offers one such model. In her study of white women in California, she found that most of the women adopted a colourblind stance, a finding that she suggests reflects the dominant attitude to race in the US. Yet she also identified a number of women who adopted the colour cognisant approach. These women were aware of race and racism in their own and others' lives, and were active in challenging it. In focusing on a range of women from different backgrounds, Frankenberg revealed a variety of attitudes in all racial groups that did away with simple correlations between whiteness and colourblindness. Using her model, white people can analyse their own behaviour and begin to move away from colourblindness and racism, without disowning their identities as white people. The central issue becomes not whiteness but racism, and the denial of its existence. This shift in focus is to some degree semantic, for it is still mainly white people who need to reconsider their colourblindness and their racism. But it does represent a more constructive approach to challenging white attitudes to race than focusing on skin colour could ever achieve.

When I reconsider my own behaviour in light of Frankenberg's framework, I can see that I began with a colourblind approach. Although I did note the children's ethnic backgrounds, I did not consider mine as having any relevance to the situation. Later, I began to see that my own racial background was an important factor in the way I saw my work and my interactions with the children, and my approach became more race cognisant. But in the difficult area of dealing with racism, I still struggled. I knew I should challenge racist attitudes, but I found it hard to do so. Why was it so difficult for me to apply the principles I sincerely believed in? One way of understanding my difficulty is to see it as an example of the fear encountered by those who attempt to shift their attitudes from colourblindness to colour and power cognisance. According to the colour cognisant approach I have not a *right* but the *duty* to confront racism. But I had internalised the old approach and I still feared that my intervention would be incompetent and counterproductive. It was only when I saw that by remaining silent I was actually supporting the continued presence of racist attitudes in the classroom, that I slowly gathered the courage to act more decisively.

Like Frankenberg, I found teachers I would describe as taking a colour and power cognisant approach alongside colleagues who were more colour and power evasive. The teachers I identified as more confident with issues of race seemed to achieve the difficult balance between recognising the significance of race in the children's lives yet not allowing it to blind them to other aspects of their identities. They had also reflected privately on the significance of race in their own lives. They did not see race, as I had, as something only the ethnic minority children would have to confront but as something that we all have to deal with, though it affects us in different – and often unjust – ways. Paula's story of her unconscious racism in Mexico illustrates how some teachers could reflect on their own experience as white people in a racialised world without letting it overshadow other aspects of their identities.

It is significant that these teachers saw teaching as a political activity. This gets to the heart of what is meant by power cognisance. They saw themselves as in a sense activists: they wanted to give children an education that would enable them to achieve a level of social, economic and personal success that their working class and ethnic minority status would otherwise deny them. These teachers were concerned with the children as individuals and rejected all attempts to generalise in any crude way, but they believed that the children's experiences and life chances were influenced by their social identities, their gender, class, ethnicity. They knew that girls are treated differently from boys in all cultures, and that less might be expected of them. They also knew that too many children from ethnic minorities and lower socio-economic groups do not achieve their full potential in school (Gillborn and Mirza, 2000). And they saw it as their job to change these realities. Other teachers who were deeply committed to the children in their care did not take that broader political view, and were perhaps less passionate about the wider implications of their work.

In the end what matters is the effect teachers' attitudes to race have on the children in their care. At St Matthew's it was felt that since the children did relatively well academically, and since friendly relations between the children and between teachers and children were a strong feature of the school, there was no particular reason to change. But the entries in my diary tell a more complicated story, revealing that many of the children felt uncomfortable talking about the differences between them, and were confused about their own identities. While aspects of their thinking were certainly influenced by home, I felt there was an important role for us as teachers in helping them to understand their developing identities, but this work was seldom done. The teachers at St Matthew's showed me that this was partly because of the pressure to adhere to a script and deliver a centrally agreed body of information, sometimes of little obvious relevance to the pupils. But I believe that there are also more uncomfortable reasons this work was left undone. As teachers we ourselves had often not done the work of understanding how race and ethnicity affected our lives, and those of the people around us.

Implications for the future

My experience suggests that there is a good deal of work to be done in re-thinking attitudes to race and to other forms of difference in our schools. There are a number of possibilities for change, and a number of different places to start.

Implications for policy

The general trend in national educational policy making in the UK and elsewhere over the past twenty years has been toward centralising control of schools (Blair and Arnot, 1993; Paterson, 2003). This has led to the dominance of one educational philosophy, which is managerialist in style (Case *et al*, 2000) and colourblind in practice (Blair and Cole, 2000; Hill, 2001). There has recently been some evidence of a greater interest in the implications of social exclusion (DfES, 2003). These initiatives do not go very far in themselves, but they may signal the development of a more inclusive approach to education.

The National Curriculum emerges from this study as the single most significant centralising force (Paterson, 2003). Gradually over the past fifteen years teaching in England has come to be seen as synonymous with delivering the National Curriculum. The content of that curriculum, aspects of which were once seen as highly contentious in its monocultural stance, is now accepted as the natural order of things. It is not just what we teach that has been determined by government but also, increasingly, how we teach it. The widely used, though non-statutory, literacy and numeracy strategies lay down a precise and uniform structure for each English and maths lesson. They specify, sometimes word for word, what teachers should say to the children, how long they should spend on each element, and what resources they should use. The effect of this level of prescription is to deskill the profession, so that teachers become operatives rather than being professionals who make complex judgements on behalf of their pupils. It seems inevitable that such prescription narrows the vision of teachers so that they become accustomed, when thinking about their teaching, to asking themselves only pragmatic questions about resource organisation and seating arrangements, rather than the more fundamental questions, such as why am I doing this? Is this what children need today?

In a system which is centred on the curriculum and not the child, it is unlikely that children who are in any way different from the majority will be adequately catered for. Any loosening of central control should certainly include a thorough re-think of the nature and indeed the purpose of a national curriculum. A less rigid form of curriculum control is not unprecedented: in Scotland the curriculum is already much less prescriptive and its assessment less intrusive than in England (Paterson, *ibid*).

The narrowness of the curriculum and the managerialist philosophy that drives it are also a feature of initial teacher education (ITE) institutions. The pressure to deliver an overcrowded curriculum dominated by the core subjects of numeracy and literacy, and accompanied by a draconian inspection regime, has transformed teacher education (Jones, 1999). As in primary schools, one key consequence of these reforms has been the marginalisation of the social and political dimension of learning.

Changes to ITE provision should not focus narrowly on race. Rather, they should seek to foster a more personally reflective, socially aware, ethically involved culture of teaching. Such a culture might provide a moral challenge to the managerialist approach to education that currently dominates. One way of encouraging reflection and the habit of linking personal experience with social patterns, would be to make a stronger connection between teachers and research. The call for teachers to be active researchers on a small or large scale has often been made (Elliott, 1993; Bullough and Pinnegar, 2001; DfEE, 2001). But teachers as readers of research would be an equally significant development. Such a change in culture would take time, resources and a good deal of direction. Recent government initiatives such as research scholarships for teachers (DfEE, 2001) and a National Teacher Research Panel suggest there is some appetite for this work.

One of the factors that militates against more sophisticated thinking on race and other social identities among teachers is the narrow range of backgrounds from which teachers themselves are drawn. I have described how working alongside a Muslim colleague, Kadeja, changed my thinking about the place of Islam in the school, and how talking to Rose and Paula made me more aware of the need to take into account the ways in which social class interrelates with race. Collaborative work of this kind can help teachers to question their assumptions and rethink taken for granted behaviour as being only one – often culturally determined – choice among many (Moore, 1999). The way my conversations with these teachers changed my thinking shows the potential that exists if the teaching profession were to become more ethnically and socially diverse.

Implications for schools

St Matthew's Primary School is depicted in this book as a school that conformed to the requirements of national government in order to avoid intervention from government inspectors. Yet even in this environment, other views were heard and alternative approaches were able to develop, albeit in a limited way. This process was illustrated most clearly by the Inclusion Week held at the school, partly in response to pressure from parents. The idea of a week of activities related to non-white achievement, though itself seriously flawed, did offer limited opportunities to address neglected issues in the curriculum, and signalled a slight change of emphasis in the school's priorities. More importantly, it demonstrated the potential for more radical action. Having allowed parents to influence the direction the school was taking, it becomes possible to imagine allowing the voices of all staff, together with parents and children, to be heard, to forge a sense of shared values that may differ from values that are centrally imposed. This is no easy matter: it is likely to lead to conflict as well as to co-operation. But these are debates that need to be aired and resolved if a shared sense of purpose is ever to be achieved.

One issue that appeared ripe for discussion among the staff at St Matthew's was gender equality, which was understood quite differently by different teachers. A debate about the problem could have been productive and could have led to a whole school agreement on a policy for tackling sexism and aggression in the school. For many teachers this was a far more pressing issue than anti-racism, even though they were connected. Yet no action was taken. I thought this was because the teachers who most wanted change were those who saw the issue primarily in racial terms, so felt unable to raise the issue publicly. A culture of openness and collegiality, and a recognition of the importance of philosophical, political and theoretical issues in teaching may help to encourage this kind of debate.

The development of such a collaborative approach to schooling has to be gradual. But another implication of this study for school policy is much more easily achievable, and perhaps more pressing. I have reflected on the inadequacy of my responses to racist incidents in the classroom, and discussed the difficulties posed by viewing the problem as a personal dilemma. While I came to understand the fear I experienced in dealing with racism as partly to do with my colourblind approach to race, it was compounded by the institutional silence on racism, which left me to confront the issue as an individual rather than within the framework of a well understood, high profile whole school policy. I know that I was not alone in feeling vulnerable in dealing with racism because there was no clearly understood policy to guide my response. Most schools have a policy on dealing with racism, but this is not enough. It must be widely debated, and frequently revisited by the entire staff body, and introduced and reinforced at regular intervals with the children, so they know what racism is and are aware of the consequences of racist behaviour long before an incident arises. The responsibility for the continuing visibility of the policy must remain with the headteacher, to ensure that the importance of the issue is understood by all (Troyna and Hatcher, 1992). Within such a supportive and enabling structure, it is likely that more teachers will feel able to confront racist incidents in their schools.

Implications for teachers

While changes at policy and school level are crucial, I have argued throughout this book that the starting point for change should be the attitudes of teachers. Having accepted that the power to determine what and how they teach is increasingly being taken away from them, this may seem unfair. Certainly this view was strongly challenged by my colleagues, most of whom felt that the main difficulties were caused by pressure exerted by central government. They argued that although part of the problem was their own lack of knowledge, they would have liked to teach more relevant material, but that they were prevented from doing so by the narrowness of the National Curriculum and the requirement to ensure the children achieved reasonable scores in national tests. For them, the starting point had to be a change in educational policy.

While policy change is certainly a key issue, there are two reasons to focus on teachers as the starting point for change. In the current political climate, it appears unlikely that major changes will be made to the direction of education policy. While we must continue to press for reform at national level, doing only this effectively means achieving nothing. So as things currently stand, a more realistic focus for change is individual teachers (Moore, 1999). Second, as my diary entries show, the day to day interactions between teachers and children exert just as powerful an influence on children's ideas about race and identity as the formal curriculum. It is partly teachers' own unexamined preconceptions and assumptions that are responsible for some of the problems that exist in the classroom.

Many teachers need to improve their understanding of how race affects the way they teach, and their perceptions of the children in their classes. And in order to do this they need to understand how their own lives have been influenced by race. That is no easy task.

For me, the first step to acknowledging the significance of race was keeping a diary. Another way to gain a sense of your own ideas is by comparing them with those of others. We can only really know what we think when we articulate it, either in writing or in speech. And secondly, it becomes much easier to see one's own point of view as one among many when engaged in discussions with valued and trusted friends or colleagues. But the insecurity I and many of my colleagues felt in discussing race suggests that this degree of openness requires an enormous amount of trust.

This conception of our own opinion as one among many rather than as the accepted view on something has important consequences in the classroom which extend beyond issues of race. It may lead to the development of a more complex and critical approach to teaching and learning in general. Giroux (1991) advocates that teachers develop the habit of offering students a chance to study material that relates to difference in its widest sense, and to be taught to read texts written by those with and without power, and to see them as products of their time and place. Such work can be also be undertaken with young children (Burgess-Macey, 1992; Epstein, 1993), though it necessitates a radical change in the way we teach. Roth (1992) suggests that teachers need to be aware that a tendency to summarise and simplify concepts and ideas for children may convey a sense of these concepts as uncontested or, worse, incontestable. We should instead make explicit the controversy, dissent and bias in all fields of study. While the National Curriculum does not encourage this approach, it does not preclude it either. Opportunities do exist for reflective teachers to present a more open and critical approach to the material they bring to the classroom than pertains today.

Perhaps the most significant implication of this book for individual teachers is the importance of personal reflection. As a white teacher from a monocultural background, teaching a Eurocentric curriculum and surrounded by white colleagues, I had little reason to question what I was doing. Yet having been given the opportunity to analyse my thinking and behaviour over a long period of time, I have been able to see what had previously been invisible to me: the impact of race – and in particular my own race – on the teaching and learning process.

Because of the recent changes in the professional lives of teachers which have begun to seep into the culture of teaching, this habit of reflection is becoming harder to sustain in the teaching profession. The shift in control of the teaching process from educationalists to policy makers, and the sheer volume of work teachers are required to do, now mean that many teachers do not take time to reflect on their teaching and the children's leaning. In particular, the habit of reflecting on how teachers' own biographies impact on the learning process is barely a feature of teacher education, though innovative teacher educators continue to call for this to change (King, 2001).

Conducting research into one's own practice in the classroom enables teachers to gain a degree of distance from their own thinking and behaviour, so that they can understand, analyse and ultimately change it (Brown and Jones, 2001). The process of writing down one's experiences and thoughts and analysing that writing over time is one way of (re)gaining control of the teaching process, of slowing down time to enable one to act more thoughtfully in the classroom. By gaining a degree of distance from our practice through writing, we teachers can uncover our unspoken assumptions about ourselves, our work and our pupils. This is crucial in practitioner research in general but it has additional significance in a project concerning whiteness which by its very nature is an identity that is rarely made explicit.

Learning to see how my race influenced my behaviour and perceptions was a lengthy process, but it is one that all teachers need to go through. Because whiteness is rarely acknowledged as a racial identity, that process is likely to be more difficult for white teachers – and is all the more vital for that. Many more children like those who appear on these pages will be growing up confused and fearful, or resentful and angry, if this critical work is avoided any longer.

References

Abbas, T. (2002) Teacher Perceptions of South Asians in Birmingham Schools and Colleges, *Oxford Review of Education*, vol 28, no 4

Ask, K. And Tjomsland, M. (1998) *Women and Islamisation – contemporary dimensions of discourse on gender relations.* Oxford, New York: Berg

Basit, T. (1997) *Eastern Values, Western Milieu: identities and aspirations of adolescent British Muslim Girls.* Aldershot: Ashgate

Baumann, G., (1996) *Contesting Culture: discourses of identity in multi-ethnic London.* Cambridge: Cambridge University Press

Baumann, G. (1999) *The Multicultural Riddle – rethinking national, ethnic and religious identities.* London: Routledge

Bhatti, G. (1999) *Asian Children at Home and at School.* London: Routledge

Bigger, J. (2000) Race Awareness and School Ethos: Reflections of School Management Issues, in: M. Leicester *et al* (eds) *Institutional Issues – Pupils, Schools and Teacher Education.* London: Falmer

Blair, M. and Arnot, M. (1993) Black and Antiracist Perspectives on the National Curriculum and Government Education Policy, in: A. King and M. Reiss (eds) (1993) *The Multicultural Dimension of the National Curriculum.* London: Falmer

Blair, M. and Cole, M. (2000) Racism and Education – The Imperial Legacy in: M. Cole (ed.) *Education, Equality and Human Rights.* London: Routledge/Falmer

Blauner, R. (1994) Talking Past Each Other: black and white languages of race in: F.L. Pincus and H.J. Ehrlich (eds) (1994) *Race and ethnic conflict : contending views on prejudice, discrimination, and ethnoviolence.* Bolder, Oxford: Westview Press

Bonnett, A. (2000) *White Identities.* Harlow: Pearson

Brown, T. and Jones, L. (2001) *Action Research and Postmodernism: Congruence and Critique.* Buckingham: Open University Press

Bullough, R.V. and Pinnegar, S.(2001) Guidelines for Quality in Autobiographical Forms of Self-Study Research, *Educational Researcher*, vol 30, no 3

Burgess-Macey, C. (1992) Tackling Racism and Sexism in the Primary Classroom, in: D. Gill, B. Mayor and M. Blair (eds) *Racism and Education – Structures and Strategies.* Buckingham: Open University Press

Case, P., Case, S. and Catling, S. (2000) Please show You're Working: a critical assessment of the impact of OFSTED inspection on primary teachers, *British Journal of Sociology of Education*, vol 21, no 4

Clancy, A., Hough, M., Ausr, R. and Kershaw, C. (2001) *Crime, Policing and Justice: the experience of ethnic minorities: Findings from the 2000 British Crime Survey.* Home Office Research Study, 223

Clandinin, J. D. and Connelly, F. M. (2000) *Narrative Inquiry – experience and story in qualitiative research.* San Francisco: Jossey Bass

Cline, T., de Abreu, G., Fihosy, C., Gray, H., Lambert, H. and Neale, J. (2002) Minority Ethnic Pupils in Mainly White Schools, *DfES Research Brief No. 365.* Nottingham: DfES Publications

Cohen, P. (1992) Hidden Narratives in Theories of Racism, in: Donald, J. And Rattansi, A. (eds) (1992) *Race, Culture and Difference.* London: Sage/OUP

Cole, M. (1992) British Values, Liberal Values or Values of Justice and Equality, in: J. Lynch, C. Modgil and S. Modgil (eds) *Cultural Diversity in Schools, vol 3: Equity or Excellence? Education and Cultural Reproduction.* London: Falmer

Commission on British Muslims and Islamophobia (2004) *Islamophobia – issues, challenges, action,* compiled by Robin Richardson, Stoke on Trent: Trentham

Connolly, P. (1998) *Racism, Gender Identities and Young Children – social relations in the multi-ethnic inner city primary school.* London: Routledge

Convery, A. (1996) Identity Issues in the Conduct and Reporting of Research, un-published PhD thesis, University of East Anglia

Crick, B. (1998) *Education for Citizenship and the Teaching of Democracy in Schools.* London: QCA

Department for Education and Employment (2001) *Best Practice Research Scholar-ships – Guidance.* London: HMSO

Department for Education and Skills (2003) *Aiming High: Raising the Achievement of Minority Ethnic Pupils.* London: HMSO

Dyer, R. (1997) *White.* London: Routledge

Dubois, W.E.B. (1998) The Souls of White Folk, in: D. Roediger (ed.) (1998) *Black on White: Black Writers on What it Means to be White.* New York: Schocken Books

Elliott, J. (1993) *Reconstructing Teacher Education.* London: Falmer

England, J. (2003) Researching race in school: a psychoanalytical perspective. Un-published PhD thesis, Manchester Metropolitan University

Epstein, D. (1993) *Changing Classroom Cultures – anti-racism, politics and schools.* Stoke-on-Trent: Trentham

Fawsi El-Solh, C. And Mabro, J. (eds) (1994) *Muslim Women's Choices.* Providence, Oxford: Berg

Francis, B. (1998) *Power Plays: primary school children's constructions of gender, power and adult work.* Stoke on Trent: Trentham

Frankenberg, R. (1993) *White Women, Race Matters.* Minneapolis: Routledge

Frankenberg, R. (1997) Introduction: Localizing Whiteness, in: *Displacing Whiteness – essays in social and cultural criticism.* Durham, London: Duke University Press

Gaine, C. (2001) 'If it's not hurting it's not working': teaching teachers about race, *Research Papers in Education,* vol 16, no.1

Gillborn, D. (1990) *Race, Ethnicity and Education- teaching and learning in multi-ethnic schools.* London: Unwin Hyman

Gillborn, D. (1996) Student Roles and Perspectives in Anti-racist education: a crisis of white ethnicity? *British Educational Research Journal* vol 22, no 2

Gillborn, D. (2001) Racism, Policy and the (mis)education of Black children in: R. Majors (ed.) *Educating Our Black Children – new directions and radical approaches.* London: Routledge

Gillborn, D. and Mirza, H.S. (2000) *Education and Inequality: Mapping Race, Class and Gender.* London: Ofsted

Gillborn, D. and Youdell, D. (2000) *Rationing Education- Policy, Practice, Reform and Equity.* Buckingham: Open University Press

Giroux, H.A. (1991) Democracy and the Discourse of Cultural Difference: towards a politics of border pedagogy, *British Journal of Sociology of Education*, vol 12, no 4

Goldberg, D. T. (2002) *The Racial State.* Malden, Oxford: Blackwell

Haque, Z. (1999) Exploring the validity and possible causes of the apparently poor performance of Bangladeshi students in British secondary schools, unpublished PhD thesis, University of Cambridge

Hernandez Sheets, R. (2000) Advancing the Field or Taking Centre Stage: the white movement in multicultural education, *Educational Researcher*, December

Hill, D. (2001) The National Curriculum, the Hidden Curriculum and Equality in: D. Hill and M. Cole, *Schooling and Equality – Fact, Concept and Policy.* London: Kogan Page

Holly, M.L. (1989) *Writing to Grow – Keeping a Personal-Professional Journal.* Portsmouth, New Hampshire: Heinemann

hooks, b. (1992) *Black Looks – Race and Representation.* Boston: South End Press

Hunter, M.L and Nettles, K.D. (1999) What About the White Women? Racial Politics in a Women's Studies Classroom, *Teaching Sociology*, vol 27

Islam Awareness Project (2003) *Discover Islam.* London: MP Media

Jeffcoate, R. (1986) Combatting Racism in: L. Cohen and A. Cohen (eds) *Multicultural Education – a Sourcebook for Teachers.* London: Harper and Row

Jones, R. (1999) *Teaching Racism or Tackling It?* Trentham Books: Stoke on Trent

King, J.E. (2001) Dyconscious Racism: Ideology, Identity and the Miseducation of Teachers, in: E. Cashmore and J. Jennings (eds) *Racism: Essential Readings.* London: Sage

Levine-Rasky, C. (2000) Framing Whiteness: working through the Tensions in introducing Whiteness to Educators, *Race, Ethnicity and Education*, vol 3, no 3

Mac an Ghaill, M. (1994) *The Making of Men.* Buckingham: Open University Press

Mac an Ghaill, M. (1999) *Contemporary Racisms and Ethnicities – social and cultural transformations.* Buckingham: Open University Press

Macpherson, W. (1999) *The Stephen Lawrence Inquiry.* London: HMSO

McIntosh, P. (1992) White Privilege and Male Privilege: a personal account of coming to see correspondences through work in Women's Studies in: M Andersen and P. Hill Collins (eds): *Race, Class and Gender, an Anthology.* Belmont: Wadsworth

Modood (1992) British Muslims and The Rushdie Affair, in: J. Donald and A. Rattansi (eds) *'Race', Culture and Difference.* London: Sage

Moore, A. (1999) *Teaching Multicultured Students – culturalism and anti-culturalism in school classrooms.* London: Falmer

Moore, A., Edwards, G., Halpin, D. and George R. (2002) Compliance, Resistance and Pragmatism: the (re)construction of schoolteacher identities in a period of intensive educational reform, *British Educational Research Journal*, vol 28, no 4

Omi, M. and Winant, H. (1986) *Racial Formation in the USA: 1960s to 1980s*. New York: Routledge and Kegan Paul

Paterson, L. (2003) The Three Educational Ideologies of the British Labour Party, 1997-2001, *Oxford Review of Education*, vol 29, no 2

Pearce, S. (2003) Compiling the White Inventory: the practice of whiteness in a British Primary School, *Cambridge Journal of Education*, vol 33, no 2

Renck Jalongo, M. and Isenberg, J. (1995) *Teachers' Stories – from personal narrative to professional insight*. San Francisco: Jossey-Bass

Roth, J. (1992) Of What Help is He? a review of Foucault and education, *American Educational Research Journal*, vol 29, no 4

Said, E. W. (1978) *Orientalism*. London: Routledge and Kegan Paul

Said, E.W. (1993) *Culture and Imperialism*. London: Chatto and Windus

Sarup, M. (1991) *Education and the Ideologies of Racism*. Stoke on Trent: Trentham

Scottish Executive Education Department (2001) *Anti-Racist Toolkit*, Retrieved: 3rd April 2005 from www.antiracisttoolkit.org.uk

Sewell, T. (1997) *Black Masculinities and Schooling – how black boys survive modern schooling*. Stoke on Trent: Trentham

Shain, F. (2003) *The Schooling and Identity of Asian Girls*. Stoke on Trent: Trentham

Spivak, G.C. and Harasym, S. (1990) *Gayatri Chakravorty Spivak, The Postcolonial Critic- Interviews, Strategies, Dialogues*. London: Routledge

Troyna, B. (1998) 'The Whites of my Eyes, Nose, Ears...' A Reflexive Account of 'whiteness' in race-related research, in: P. Connolly and B. Troyna (eds) (1998) *Researching Racism in Education – politics, theory and practice*. Buckingham: Open University Press

Troyna, B. and Hatcher, R. (1992) *Racism in Children's Lives – a study of mainly white primary schools*. London: Routledge

Yamani, M. (ed) (1996) *Feminism and Islam – legal and literary perspectives*. Reading: Ithaca

Youdell, D. (2003) Identity Traps or How Black Students Fail: the interactions between biographical, sub-cultural and learner identities, *British Journal of Sociology of Education*, vol 24, no 1

Young, L. (2000) Imperial Culture – the primitive, the savage and white civilisation in: L. Back and J. Solomos (eds), *Theories of Race and Racism, a Reader*. London: Routledge

Zine, J. (2000) Redefining Resistance: towards an Islamic subculture in schools, *Race, Ethnicity and Education*, vol 3, no 3

Index

Index